D.

Collins

Student Support
Materials for
AQA A2 Sociology

Unit 3

Beliefs in Society

Liz Steel
r Langley

Religious, political and scientific belief systems

Belief systems

A belief system is any integrated set of ideas, which influences the way that people see the world. Belief systems can take several forms but the most important types are religious, political and scientific.

Religious belief systems

Religion can be difficult to define, but any definition is usually based on a belief in the existence of a supernatural entity or other forces. Religions may or may not claim the existence of a supreme God or several gods.

Type of religion	Examples
Monotheistic – belief in a single God	Christianity, Islam and Judaism
Polytheistic – belief in several gods	Hinduism and the religions of the ancient Greeks and Romans
Spiritual religion without a belief in god	Buddhism does not involve a belief in the existence of a god but it has a set of values by which people are expected to live their lives
Cult with supernatural beliefs but no concept of god	Heaven's Gate cult, which believed that humans were merely vehicles carrying the souls of interstellar travellers. Members of the sect committed suicide in order to join a spacecraft which they believed was travelling behind a comet

Table 1
Types of religion

Two different approaches have been taken to identifying and defining religions and distinguishing them from non-religious belief systems.

Substantive definitions – these are concerned with the content of religion. Yinger (1961) defined religion as 'a system of beliefs and practices by means of which a group of people struggles with the ultimate problems of human life'.

Functional definitions – these define religion in terms of the functions it performs for society and for individuals. For example, Durkheim (1961) defined religion in terms of a distinction between two domains in the world, one of which is **sacred** and the other **profane**. Things in the sacred domain produce a sense of awe and respect, whereas the profane does not. Durkheim even thought that nationalism was a type of religion – he called it a **civil religion**, because it had similar functions to more conventional religions.

The idea of civil religion has been particularly criticised for stretching the definition to include beliefs that have no supernatural element to them. While there might be similarities between nationalism and religion, beliefs such as nationalism do not provide ultimate meanings about the purpose of life, nor do they explain the origins of the universe as many religions claim to.

Examiners' notes

This material provides the starting point for answers to questions about different types of religion, but for many questions you will also need to use the sections on religious organisations.

Examiners' notes

In 18- and 33-mark questions on religion it may sometimes be necessary to discuss the definition of religion.

Essential notes

Functional definitions tend to be too inclusive (it is too easy to qualify as a religion); while substantive ones tend to be too exclusive (it is too difficult to qualify as a religion).

Religious belief systems remain dominant in some parts of the world, although in Western societies alternative belief systems have become more influential since the 18th century.

Political belief systems

Political belief systems are based upon views about how society should be organised and do not have a supernatural element. Nevertheless, political beliefs can be so strongly held that they lead to violence, wars and the persecution of social groups.

Examples of political belief systems include a belief in **free market capitalism** (sometimes called neo-liberalism), **Marxism**, socialism, liberalism and so on.

Communism was influential in the Soviet Union from 1917 to 1990. Communists believed that the **means of production**, e.g. land and factories, should be run by the state rather than owned by individuals, to create greater equality.

Fascism was influential in Nazi Germany from 1933 to 1945. Proponents believed that the interests of the state should be paramount, and that this required the leadership of an authoritarian dictator who pursued the interests of the nation.

Neo-liberalism (belief in free markets) is influential in the contemporary USA. Neo-liberals believe that private enterprise is the best way to run society, and that competition drives efficiency and ensures consumers' needs are met.

Scientific belief systems

Scientific belief systems have their basis in the belief that it is possible to understand the natural world and produce truthful knowledge about it. They can be used to justify certain types of behaviour and to criticise others, e.g. behaviour relating to health.

Objectivity, values and ideology

Bierstedt (1963) defines **objectivity** as meaning that 'the conclusions arrived at as the result of enquiry or investigation are independent of the race, colour, creed, occupation, nationality, religion, moral preference, and political predisposition of the investigator'.

In contrast, **value-laden** beliefs are influenced by the moral preferences of an individual and are at least partly **subjective** – based on personal opinion, not unbiased truth.

Generally the followers of religious, political and scientific belief systems do not believe them to be value-laden but see them as objective. However, others may well see them as biased ideologies.

An **ideology** can be defined as a belief system that supports the interests of a particular social group at the expense of others. Ideologies can be used to maintain the power of a dominant group in society. Religious, political and scientific belief systems have all been seen as ideological.

Examiners' notes

You are unlikely to get a full 18- or 33-mark question just about political beliefs but you may be able to use this knowledge as part of the answer to a longer question.

Essential notes

Whether a belief system is an ideology, or fundamentally true, is often contested. Marxists and feminists tend to regard all religions as ideological. Most scientists see science as pursuing truth independent of the values of individuals, but some sociologists argue that science too is value-laden.

Marxism and neo-Marxism

Introduction

There are a number of different perspectives on ideology. All agree that there are major belief systems in society, which are shaped by the interests of powerful groups, but they disagree about who the powerful groups are, and about the extent of their influence on beliefs.

Marxism and ideology

Marxists argue that capitalist and other class-based societies are dominated by a **ruling-class ideology** – a set of beliefs that supports the interests of the dominant economic class in society.

Marxists believe that capitalist societies are divided into two classes.

1. The dominant **ruling class** or **bourgeoisie** who own the means of production such as capital, machinery, land and labour power.
2. A **subject class** which does not own the means of production and therefore has to work for the ruling class in order to survive.

The structure of society has two parts:

a. The **economic base**, which includes the means of production and is controlled by the ruling class.
b. The **superstructure**, which includes all the non-economic parts of society including the state, the mass media, education and religion.

The Marxist perspective argues that the ruling class exploit the subject class and attempt to maintain their dominance over them by controlling the ideas, beliefs and values of society.

In *The German Ideology* (1846) Marx and Engels argued that: 'The ideas of the ruling class, are, in every age, the ruling ideas.'

Marxists believe that in capitalist societies the dominant ideology is reproduced partly through the mass media. This encourages:

- acceptance of capitalism as the best or only viable economic system
- acceptance of the power of the capitalist state
- a **consumer culture** to consume the products of capitalism to make profits for companies
- a passive workforce which does not question its low wages.

Neo-Marxism and ideology

Neo-Marxists tend to believe that the original Marxist view of ideology – that the beliefs of all members of society are directly determined by the economic system – is too **deterministic**.

Some of the later writings of Marx suggest that the economic base of society influences or limits people's values and beliefs in society, but does not directly determine them. Neo-Marxists have therefore developed less deterministic views of ideology.

Examiners' notes

Look out for 18- or 33-mark questions about the influence of ruling-class ideology in society today. Balance the Marxist view with other viewpoints such as neo-Marxism, feminism and postmodernism.

Examiners' notes

You can draw upon your knowledge of education (if you studied that for Unit 2) to illustrate the Marxist view of ideology.

Essential notes

Neo-Marxists have tried to update the ideas of Marx so that they can be applied to modern societies.

Key study
Raymond Williams: Class and ideology

Raymond Williams (1965, 1978) claimed that the ruling class has a more individualistic culture (believing people succeed by pursuing their own individual interests), while working-class culture is more **collectivist** (believing people succeed through group action, for example, a trade union going on strike).

Furthermore, ruling-class ideology is not always dominant but can be challenged by **residual ideology** (the ideology of a declining class, such as landowners in Britain) and **emergent ideology** (the ideology of a new class that is developing, such as rich celebrities).

Residual and emergent ideologies may be **oppositional** (opposed to the dominant culture) or **alternative** (they coexist with the dominant culture).

Key study
Antonio Gramsci: Dual consciousness

Antonio Gramsci (1971) argued that members of society possess **dual consciousness**. They are partly influenced by ruling-class ideology because of the media, the education system and religion, which promote it. However, they may also have direct experience of **exploitation**, for example, from poor working conditions and low wages. The working class partly see through the capitalist system, while not rejecting it altogether.

Examiners' notes

Analysing the concept of ideology by looking at these different examples can allow you to demonstrate analytical skills and help to get you into the top mark band for longer questions.

Evaluation

For Marxism/neo-Marxism	Against Marxism/neo-Marxism
The Glasgow Media Group has conducted a number of studies, which claim that the media has a consistent pro-capitalist bias.	**Postmodernists** such as Pakulski and Waters (1996) argue that classes are no longer significant so there is no longer a dominant-class ideology.
The American Marxists Bowles and Gintis (1976) claimed that the US education system created docile workers.	Feminists argue that ideology reflects patriarchal divisions rather than class divisions.
Paul Willis (1977) found that working-class lads in the British education system ensured that they got working-class jobs even though they were not completely taken in by ruling-class ideology.	Anti-racists believe that **ethnic** divisions are more important than class.

Essential notes

The Glasgow Media Group studied the coverage of strikes and industrial action and showed that management was almost always portrayed as being more reasonable than strikers in television news.

Table 2
Evidence and arguments for and against Marxism and neo-Marxism

Feminist discourse and postmodern perspectives on ideology

Feminism and ideology

Feminists believe that it is not ruling-class ideas that dominate society, but patriarchal ideas. **Patriarchy** refers to male dominance and control in society. Patriarchal ideology might involve beliefs such as:

- men are superior to women
- men are more logical than women
- women are too emotional to hold positions of responsibility
- it is natural for women to take the main responsibility for childcare.

Although feminists share the same general viewpoint, there are several different feminist perspectives, each with different views on patriarchal ideology.

Radical feminist writer Kate Millet (1970) believes men are socialised into having a dominant temperament by society's culture; however, non-ideological factors such as violence also play a part in maintaining male dominance. Germaine Greer (2000) also considers that patriarchal ideology is entrenched in society, reflected in the way women are expected to improve their physical appearance to attract men.

Socialist feminist Margaret Benston (1972) believes that the ideology, which sees women as secondary wage earners benefits both male power and capitalism, as women have less economic power than men.

Black feminist Heidi Safia Mirza (1997) considers that black women are doubly disadvantaged by racist as well as patriarchal ideology; however, some black women challenge these ideologies by working hard to succeed in education.

Criticisms of feminist views

- Valerie Bryson (1999) criticises the idea of patriarchy, arguing that it merely describes, rather than explains, gender inequality.
- Feminist views of ideology may be becoming less relevant as opportunities have increased for women and Western societies are becoming less patriarchal.

Discourse and ideology

Marxists and feminists both believe that inequality creates a dominant group, and this group then creates an ideology which supports their interests.

An alternative approach is used by discourse analysts who see beliefs as creating inequality, and not the other way round. **Discourse analysis** looks at how people exercise power by writing, thinking and talking about something in a certain way, and, in doing so, reveal their ideologies. Discourse analysis has been used to understand racist beliefs.

Examiners' notes

In essays about feminism, referring to the different types is sometimes specified as one of the criteria to attain the top mark band.

Essential notes

Feminists are also criticised for ignoring class and ethnic influences on ideology.

Key study
Edward Said: Orientalism

According to Said (1995, 1997), **Orientalism** is a discourse involving Western descriptions of the East or Orient. Orientalism sees non-Westerners as the **other** – a person who is alien to the West and very different. Western politicians, popular culture and the mass media tend to portray Orientals as belligerent, violent, primitive, cunning and untrustworthy.

Recently, in the wake of terrorist attacks such as 9/11, Orientalist ideology has been directed specifically against Islam and has helped to create **Islamophobia**.

Said did not believe there is any truth in this Orientalist ideology but saw it as a way of justifying American intervention in Islamic countries.

Evaluation of discourse analysis

Discourse analysis succeeds in showing the importance of language and the way people talk about issues for the exercise of power. It has been very useful in developing an understanding of racism.

However, sometimes it does not really explain why certain discourses are accepted and others are not. Marxists and feminists argue that the discourses of powerful groups are the ones that are accepted.

Postmodernism and ideology

Postmodernists do not generally use the term ideology. However, Lyotard's (1979) concept of **metanarrative** has a similar meaning, i.e. a 'big story' about how the world works and how it should be improved. Lyotard argued that in **modernity** metanarratives such as fascism, communism or **scientific rationalism**, which aimed to improve the world, ended in disaster; for example, the Holocaust, mass deaths under Stalin in Communist USSR and global warming. He contended that in postmodern society people no longer believe in such metanarratives and ideology is declining.

Evaluation of postmodernism

Greg Philo and David Miller (2001) believe that postmodernism itself is value-laden and a form of ideology, which supports capitalism. It celebrates the apparent acceptance of consumer culture without taking account of the fact that the poor cannot afford to consume like richer members of society, and so supports inequality.

Examiners' notes

This is a useful, alternative theory of ideology that stresses the importance of language rather than the power of particular social groups in society. You can impress the examiner by using this in longer questions on theories of ideology.

Examiners' notes

Postmodernism is also useful for evaluating the other theories since it is so different from them. If you can make it relevant, always include it as a perspective on an issue for 18- and 33-mark questions. But don't forget it has its critics as well.

Science as a belief system

Auguste Comte and stages of human development

Some sociologists have argued that **science** is a quite different type of belief system to **political ideologies** and religion. For example, the **functionalist** sociologist Auguste Comte (1830) saw society as passing through three stages progressing towards scientific knowledge:

Table 3
Comte and stages of development

Stage of development	Approximate time period	Characteristics of beliefs
Theological stage	Pre-18th century	Religious and superstitious beliefs are dominant. People believe because they have faith. They follow beliefs from sacred texts and religious leaders. Beliefs are not open to question or debate.
Metaphysical stage	18th century	Philosophical beliefs are dominant. People can now use **rationality** to decide what to believe and how to behave. For example, political philosophy led to the introduction of democracy rather than believing that kings and queens should rule by divine right.
Positive stage	19th century onwards	Science is the dominant belief system. People believe those things that can be tested and proved to be true using **objective** knowledge. Beliefs are no longer a matter of opinion.

Essential notes

Comte's framework is supported by the theory of secularisation. It can be contrasted with postmodern theories.

Examiners' notes

Use Comte's ideas as a starting point for essay questions such as those about whether science has replaced religion as an ideological influence in society.

From Comte's point of view, scientific beliefs are fundamentally different from other types of belief. They are not a matter of opinion as scientific facts are independent of the beliefs of individuals. Unlike religion, science does not rely upon faith but upon evidence. Scientific knowledge can be tested through research, and false beliefs can be rejected. A move towards a scientific belief system represents progress.

Positivism and science

Comte advocated positivism as an objective, scientific way of producing knowledge. He believed this approach could be applied to social sciences such as sociology as well as physical sciences such as chemistry, biology and physics.

The main features of positivism are:

- There are objective social facts about the social world. These facts can be expressed in statistics.

- These facts are not influenced by the researcher's personal opinion (or subjective viewpoint) or their beliefs about right and wrong (**values**) and are therefore value-free.
- You can look for **correlations** (patterns in which two or more things tend to occur together).
- Correlations may represent **causal relationships** (one thing causing another).
- It is possible to discover **laws** of human behaviour – causes of behaviour, which are true for all humans everywhere and throughout history just as there are laws in science.
- Human behaviour is shaped by **external stimuli** (things that happen to us) rather than **internal stimuli** (what goes on in the human mind).
- To be scientific you should only study what you can observe. It is therefore unscientific to study people's emotions, **meanings** or **motives**, which are internal to the unobservable mind.
- Scientific knowledge is produced through **induction**; you collect evidence and induce a theory from the evidence.

Karl Popper: Falsification and science

An alternative view of science as a belief system was put forward by Karl Popper (1959). Popper agreed with Comte that social science, unlike religion, can be objective. However, unlike Comte, he did not believe it could produce laws that will necessarily be true for all time.

He saw all science as based on **falsifiable** theories, which made precise **predictions** that could then be tested. If repeatedly tested and found to be correct, a theory may be provisionally accepted, but there is always the possibility that it will be proved wrong (or falsified) in the future.

Popper believed that sociology could be objective if it made precise predictions that could be falsified. However, he regarded some sociology, such as Marxism, as unscientific because it did not include precise predictions. For example, Marx did not produce precise predictions about when a proletarian revolution would take place.

Popper used a **deductive** approach: from the theory you deduce hypotheses and make precise predictions, then check that these are correct. (This is unlike the inductive approach of positivism, which induces theories from the data collected.) Both Popper and positivists see scientific belief systems as superior to other belief systems. However, positivists see science as producing objective truth, while Popper saw science as getting as close as possible to the truth, although it was always possible that a theory would be falsified in the future.

Science in social context

Some sociologists do not see science as being objective in the way believed by positivists and Popper. Instead, they argue that science is a belief system, like any other, which is influenced and shaped by the society in which those beliefs are produced.

Essential notes

Positivism is not universally accepted as a model of science. If anything, Popper's views on science are more widely accepted.

Essential notes

Popper did not see science as ideological – he saw it as a genuine search for the truth. However, he argued that social scientists needed to make precise predictions and be careful to make their theories falsifiable if they were to be seen as scientific.

☞ This topic continues on the next two pages

Key study
Charles Darwin: Evolution

Roger Gomm (1982) argues that Darwin's theory of **evolution** was accepted because the social context of Victorian Britain, with its **laissez-faire capitalism**, welcomed the ideas of **natural selection** and **survival of the fittest**. Opposition to social revolution encouraged acceptance of evolutionary theory, and of fossil evidence, because evolutionary thinking allowed Victorian Britons to see themselves as superior to the people in conquered colonies.

As well as being influenced by the broad social context, scientific knowledge can be influenced by the desires of scientists to have successful careers. This means that scientists may not always be objective. Kaplan (1964) distinguished between **reconstructed logics** (the methods scientists claim to use) and **logic in use** (the actual methods they use).

Michael Lynch (1983) illustrated this by showing how scientists studying rats' brains ignored slides that contradicted their theories, dismissing them as **artefacts** (or mistakes produced during the laboratory procedures). He argued that scientists look for evidence to confirm theories and ignore evidence that might falsify them. They are reluctant to accept evidence that may undermine their work.

Examiners' notes

If you get an 18-mark question on scientific beliefs, remember only 6 marks are for knowledge and understanding, while 12 are for interpretation, application, analysis and evaluation.

Key study
Thomas Kuhn: Scientific revolutions

Thomas Kuhn (1962) questioned the idea that science is objective. He believed that science operates through **paradigms** – general theories or sets of beliefs held by groups of scientists. Each scientific paradigm has a social base of the scientists who have dedicated their careers to working within it. Scientists tend to work within a single paradigm, ignoring evidence that contradicts it or does not fit the theory. Only when many inexplicable anomalies are found does a scientific revolution take place and the paradigm is replaced by a new one. An example is the replacement of Sir Isaac Newton's views of physics with Albert Einstein's theory of relativity.

Postmodernism and science

Lyotard (1984) believed that science is just another metanarrative or big story about the world, with no more validity than other metanarratives. He argued therefore that science is not different in kind from any other belief system. Different belief systems are accepted in different societies and at different stages in history, and no one belief system is superior to others.

According to Lyotard, science involves a metanarrative of progress, suggesting that humans can control and perfect the world. This view became more influential from the 18th century onwards, although it never completely replaced religion. However, in the modern era the metanarrative of progress came to dominate Western thought. Then in recent decades modernity has been replaced by **postmodernity**.

In postmodernity, people become sceptical of all metanarratives that tell them what is right and wrong, and tell them how to live their lives. Science has become discredited because it has failed to solve problems such as cancer, and it has been used in a way that creates new problems (such as nuclear weapons and global warming).

Science consists of **denotative language-games**, which are based upon whether statements are true or not. Denotative language-games have been replaced by **technical language-games**, concerned with whether things are useful rather than whether they are true.

People may therefore no longer seek the truth from one single belief system; instead they can pick and choose from a whole variety of different belief systems. These are outlined in the table below.

Examiners' notes

The ideas of postmodernists such as Lyotard contrast with all the other perspectives on belief systems, so are invaluable for giving you a chance to demonstrate analysis and evaluation skills on this and other topics.

Type of beliefs	Beliefs in previous eras	Beliefs in postmodernity
Scientific beliefs	In the modern era, scientific knowledge was accepted as the objective truth.	Science seen as just one amongst many possible truths (e.g. people use alternative therapies as well as traditional scientific medicine).
Political beliefs	Political ideologies, such as communism and fascism, had a powerful influence in modern societies.	People reject single political metanarratives but may be interested in single-issue politics (e.g. ecology, human rights or the rights of minority groups).
Religious beliefs	Religion was dominant in pre-modern societies and most people still believed in one of the dominant world religions in the modern era.	People no longer follow a single religion, but pick and choose from the variety of beliefs available in **New Age movements**, **sects** and **cults**.

Table 4
Postmodernism and the development of belief systems

Conclusion

Most sociologists agree that the degree of faith in science is influenced by social factors. However, as science allows beliefs to be tested against the evidence, the scientific beliefs that withstand testing are seen as objective truths.

However, the extent to which science has lost influence can be exaggerated. For example, most people still rely upon scientifically based healthcare and technology is integral to people's lives, although people may be more sceptical about science than they were in the past.

Functionalist views of religion

Stability and change

A variety of sociological perspectives have examined the relationship between religious beliefs, social change and stability.

Some perspectives argue that the main role of religion is to integrate groups of people and as a result religion can lead to social stability. However, other sociologists argue that religious beliefs can encourage believers to change society or lead to conflict between groups. They see religion as leading to social change rather than stability.

The functionalist perspective on religious beliefs

Functionalist analysis is concerned with the contribution an institution makes to meeting society's needs. From a functionalist perspective, religion contributes to meeting society's needs through providing a shared **culture**, particularly shared moral values, thereby creating harmony and integration.

Émile Durkheim: Religion and social solidarity

Durkheim (1912) noted that all societies distinguish between:

- **sacred** objects, rituals and people, which are regarded as having special significance and are treated with awe and veneration

  and

- **profane** objects, activities and people, which are ordinary, everyday and not treated as special.

However, Durkheim believed there was nothing intrinsically special about sacred objects. Instead, they are made special because they are symbolic of or represent a particular social group.

In his study of Australian Aborigines, Durkheim found that each group had its own totem, an object from the natural world, which they worshipped. The totem represented the social group and he therefore argued that, in worshipping their totem, people were in fact worshipping society.

The main role of religion is to reinforce shared values and moral beliefs. This helps to strengthen the **collective conscience**, or the conscience of society. By defining the shared values as sacred, religion gives those values greater power.

Through acts of collective worship, members of society express approval of the moral bonds that unite them. Through such acts as singing or chanting they feel a sense of belonging to society. Religion therefore strengthens **social solidarity** and creates a sense of unity and belonging in society.

Durkheim uses an **inclusive** definition of religion (see pp 4–5). He saw nationalism as a type of **civil religion** because he believed it performed the same functions – it united people with shared beliefs and rituals. Singing the national anthem is an example of a unifying nationalistic experience.

Examiners' notes

A nine-mark question may ask you to identify and explain three functions of religion, or an 18- or 33-mark question may ask you to assess the view that religion promotes social solidarity.

Essential notes

Durkheim admitted that with education providing moral values to an increasing extent, religion might lose some of its influence, but he still thought there was 'something eternal in religion' so it would never die out entirely.

Key study

Bronisław Malinowski: Religion in the Trobriand Islands

Malinowski (1954) was an anthropologist who conducted a functionalist study of the role of religion in the Trobriand Islands. Malinowski saw religion as crucial to helping people deal with situations of emotional stress that threaten social solidarity. This emotional stress might come from two sources:

1. Anxiety and tension from **life crises** such as birth, puberty, marriage and death. The emotion produced by these events can make it difficult for individuals to continue contributing to society, and therefore all these events are accompanied by a religious ritual. Funerals, for example, provide an opportunity for the social group to express support for the bereaved and help them reintegrate into society.
2. Unpredictable events and circumstances, which produce tension and anxiety. These also tend to be accompanied by religious rituals that provide feelings of confidence and control and so help reduce anxiety. For example, in the Trobriand Islands, religious rituals were performed before the islanders went fishing in canoes in dangerous and unpredictable deep sea waters, but there were no religious rituals when they fished in the relatively calm and safe inland lagoons.

Talcott Parsons: Religion and the value consensus

Parsons argued that religious beliefs provide guidelines for human action and standards against which people's conduct can be evaluated. Parsons argued that in the USA, Christian religious beliefs underpin the **value consensus** even for those who are not Christians because formal laws and **norms** have their origin in Christianity. The Ten Commandments, for example, provide the basis for many social norms.

Another main function of religion for Parsons was to provide a range of answers to questions about suffering, evil, the purpose of existence and so on. Religion helps society to run smoothly and prevents conflict.

Evaluation of functionalism

Functionalists identify an importance aspect of religion, the way it can unite and integrate a group of people. However, critics argue that they ignore the possibility that religion can have other effects or functions and their views may not be applicable to all societies, e.g. disagreement between religions can cause conflict; feminists argue that religion maintains patriarchy; and Marxists claim it benefits the ruling class over others.

Essential notes

Although Durkheim and Malinowski used examples from simple societies, functionalists argue that religion carries out the same basic functions in society today.

Examiners' notes

You should try to mention Durkheim, Malinowski and Parsons in any essay questions on functionalism and religion.

Examiners' notes

For an essay on functionalism flesh out these points using the material on the different perspectives and also discuss how religion can cause social change and conflict. You might also introduce neo-Marxism and postmodernism.

Marxist and neo-Marxist views of religion

The Marxist model of society

According to Marxists, in all non-**communist** societies, a **ruling class** own the means of production and from their wealth derive **power**, which allows them to control the superstructure of society. (The **superstructure** is the non-economic parts of society such as education, the state, the mass media, **religion** and beliefs, attitudes and values.)

From this point of view, religion is used to promote the interests of the ruling class by being used to support **ruling-class ideology**. Ruling-class ideology keeps the ruling class in power by discouraging subject classes from realising they are being exploited and then trying to overthrow ruling-class power.

Religion as the 'opium of the masses'

Marx (1842) famously described religion as the 'opium of the masses'. By this he meant that he saw religion as being like a drug that distorts reality and helps individuals deal with pain. He gave several examples of how religion does this.

- It promises eternal life in heaven for those who follow and accept the beliefs of a religion.
- It makes a virtue out of suffering and oppression, as in the biblical quote that 'it is easier for a camel to pass through the eye of a needle, than for a rich man to enter the Kingdom of Heaven'. Injustices during life will be rectified in the afterlife, therefore there is no need to try to overcome injustice now.
- It offers hope of supernatural intervention to end suffering. For example, Jehovah's Witnesses believe that judgement day will arrive and those who are not religious will be judged and punished.

Religion justifies and legitimates the existing social order. For example, in medieval Europe, kings and queens ruled by divine right; they got their legitimacy from God. Individuals were persuaded to accept their situation as it was divinely ordained and therefore something they should not challenge.

Religion and alienation

Marx saw religion as a form of **alienation**. Humans invent an alien being, God, which they believe to be all-powerful and to have control over them. In doing so, they give up their own true humanity by denying themselves the right to make their own decisions.

Religion as social control

Marx therefore saw religion as a mechanism of **social control**. It creates **false class consciousness** – mistaken beliefs about the true nature of social life, which justify the position of the ruling class. This prevents the working class developing **class consciousness**, in which they become aware that they are exploited, and unite to overthrow the capitalist system that exploits them.

Examiners' notes

The Marxist view of religion could form the basis of an essay question in its own right. You could be asked to compare it with another perspective, such as functionalism or feminism, or to answer questions about religion and social change or religion and conflict.

Essential notes

In the Soviet Union under communist leadership from 1917 to 1990 the state consistently opposed the existence of religious beliefs and destroyed many Russian Orthodox churches, as well as mosques and synagogues.

Marx believed that with the advent of communism, religion would no longer be necessary. Since the means of production would be communally owned by all members of society, no individuals would own this wealth and power and there would be no social **classes**. Without classes there would be no need for religion, as its sole purpose was to **legitimate** ruling class power. Religion would therefore disappear.

Evidence for the Marxist view of religion

A number of examples can be used to support the Marxist view of religion.

Example	Description	How it supports the Marxist view
Slavery	In slave societies (e.g. sugar plantations in the West Indies) slave masters tried to convert African slaves to European religions.	Slave masters saw religion as a way of controlling their slaves, preventing rebellions by giving the masters control over the slaves' beliefs.
The Hindu caste system	In the traditional Hindu caste system in India (now illegal), people were divided into five castes based upon their supposed degree of religious purity. The Brahmins (priests) were at the top and the Untouchables (unskilled labourers) at the bottom.	Since no movement was permitted between castes, this system ensured the ruling class maintained their power and control and justified the lowly position of those at the bottom in terms of their religious impurity.
The New Christian Right	Very religious Christians in the United States with highly conservative and pro-capitalist views (e.g. President George W. Bush).	The New Christian Right justify free-market capitalism, which supports the interests of the bourgeoisie, in religious terms, thereby legitimating ruling-class power.
Evangelical Christianity in Latin America	The New Christian Right have encouraged the spread of Protestant religious beliefs in predominantly Catholic Latin American countries, particularly amongst the poor in shantytowns.	Protestant religious beliefs provide religious discipline and hope of salvation in the afterlife to some of the poorest in Latin American societies, discouraging them from supporting radical Catholic liberation theology and encouraging support for US-style capitalist values.

Table 5
Examples of religious oppression that support the Marxist view

Essential notes

Communist regimes that still exist, such as that in Cuba, have come to accept that religion is going to coexist with communism, and no longer try to suppress it.

Examiners' notes

The example of Hinduism provides a useful cross-cultural example.

Examiners' notes

Remember that you are most likely to get into the top mark band if you can provide a balanced discussion of arguments for and against a perspective. These examples illustrate and support the Marxist viewpoint.

This topic continues on the next two pages

Examiners' notes

For a full essay on the Marxist view of religion you can expand on these points using material from other sections.

Criticisms of the Marxist view of religion

Marxist theories of religion have been criticised from a wide range of perspectives.

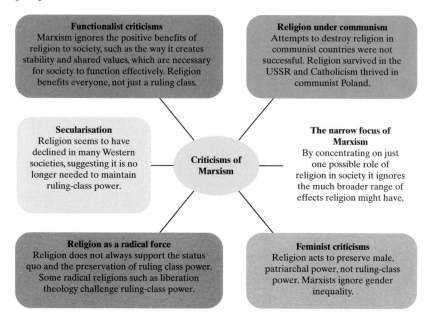

Functionalist criticisms
Marxism ignores the positive benefits of religion to society, such as the way it creates stability and shared values, which are necessary for society to function effectively. Religion benefits everyone, not just a ruling class.

Religion under communism
Attempts to destroy religion in communist countries were not successful. Religion survived in the USSR and Catholicism thrived in communist Poland.

Secularisation
Religion seems to have declined in many Western societies, suggesting it is no longer needed to maintain ruling-class power.

Criticisms of Marxism

The narrow focus of Marxism
By concentrating on just one possible role of religion in society it ignores the much broader range of effects religion might have.

Religion as a radical force
Religion does not always support the status quo and the preservation of ruling class power. Some radical religions such as liberation theology challenge ruling-class power.

Feminist criticisms
Religion acts to preserve male, patriarchal power, not ruling-class power. Marxists ignore gender inequality.

Fig. 1
Criticisms of the Marxist view of religion

Key study
Friedrich Engels: Religion as a radical force

Marx's friend and collaborator, Engels (1957), recognised religion did not always act as a conservative force supporting the interests of the ruling class. He believed that religion usually started off amongst oppressed groups in society as a way of coping with their oppression. He also argued that eventually religion could become a force for change. By uniting an oppressed group and giving them a common set of beliefs it provided the basis for future actions. When Engels wrote about early Christian sects who were opposed to Roman rule, he compared them to communist and socialist political movements campaigning for freedom from oppression. In these cases, religion became a source of resistance to oppressors and therefore a force for change.

Neo-Marxism

Neo-Marxists are new Marxists who are strongly influenced by the writings of Karl Marx but who do not agree with all aspects of them. Neo-Marxists therefore developed new theories, which diverge to some extent from Marx's original writings. In particular, they often do not agree that parts of the superstructure are completely controlled by the ruling class.

Otto Maduro: The relative autonomy of religion

Otto Maduro (1982) believes that religion has some independence or **relative autonomy** from ruling-class control and from the economic system. He denies that religion is always a **conservative force** and says that it can sometimes become revolutionary.

He uses the example of **liberation theology** to illustrate his point. Until recent decades, the Catholic Church in Latin America sided with the **bourgeoisie** and right-wing military dictatorships in Latin American countries such as El Salvador and Nicaragua. The Catholic Church gave little support to trade unions, strikers and opposition political parties. Increasingly, however, Catholic priests began to speak up for the interests of the poor. Some priests developed a new theology, which interpreted Christianity as being on the side of oppressed groups and as supporting their liberation. Liberation theology therefore developed, which argued that power and wealth, especially land, should be redistributed from the rich to the poor.

This set of religious beliefs has developed an ideology similar to Marxism whereby it encourages revolution rather than acts as the opium of the masses.

There are other instances where religion has become a radical force. For example, Cargo **cults** on islands colonised by Europeans in the Pacific believed that ships bearing a cargo of riches would appear over the horizon to give them as much wealth as their European colonisers, and this would result in the Europeans being thrown off the islands. When the ships did not appear, the cults became radical political movements seeking the expulsion of colonial occupiers.

Evaluation of neo-Marxism

There is plenty of evidence to support the neo-Marxist view that religion is not always a conservative force supporting the interests of the ruling class. Religion has quite often acted as a radical force resulting in social changes. Ironically, religion has also acted as a radical force for the overthrow of communism. In Poland in the 1990s the ruling Communist Party was opposed by free trade unions and by the Roman Catholic Church. Eventually this led to the overthrow of the communist system and its replacement by a Western democratic regime.

Conclusion

Marxist and neo-Marxist theories successfully explain the role of religion in some societies at some times, but do not explain how religion works in all societies at all times. Religion is not necessarily an expression of ruling-class ideology or revolutionary political force, although it does sometimes act in this way, as examples may illustrate.

Examiners' notes

Maduro and the example of liberation theology are very useful for discussing a range of questions including those on religion and social change, religion and conflict and religion as a conservative force.

Examiners' notes

See pp 22–29 for more on the issue of religion as a force for change. Introducing more complexity allows more analysis and helps get you into the top mark band.

Feminist views of religion

Feminism and other perspectives

Like Marxists, feminists believe that religion does not serve the interests of society as a whole but rather serves the interests of a particular social group.

Most feminists agree with Marxists that religion tends to be a force preventing change and maintaining the power of the most powerful group in society, but they see this group as being men rather than the ruling-class. They view religion as **patriarchal**, male-dominated, and serving the interests of men.

The origins of gender inequality in religion

Karen Armstrong (1993) argues that religion has not always been patriarchal. She claims that in early history women were considered central to spirituality and archaeologists have found numerous symbols of the Great Mother Goddess. In comparison there were few portrayals of male gods.

It was only around 1750 BC in Babylon that the importance of the goddess declined as the male god Marduk replaced the female goddess Tiamat as the dominant figure in religion. With the advent of Judaism, Christianity and Islam, **monotheistic** religions (which believe in one God rather than many) largely replaced **polytheistic** religions (which believed in many gods and goddesses). In all these cases God was portrayed as a male.

Gender inequality in major religions

Jean Holm (1994) argues that in the **public sphere** of religion, where important positions are held and public pronouncements are made, men almost always dominate. However, in the **private sphere**, for example the **socialisation** of children into a religion within families, women are dominant and do most of the religious work. Holm has identified inequalities between men and women in all major world religions. These are outlined in table 6.

Essential notes

These examples suggest that religion does not have to be patriarchal and that patriarchal religions are a product of the wider patriarchal society in which they are found.

Examiners' notes

Holm acknowledges that the position of women has improved in some religions. This demonstrates a liberal feminist perspective – it is important to mention different types of feminism to get into the top band for essay questions.

Examiners' notes

These examples of ways in which women can be discriminated against in religion could be useful in many of the questions in this exam.

Religion	Nature and extent of inequality
Christianity/ Roman Catholicism	God is portrayed as male and as a father figure. Jesus and all his disciples were male and the Bible was entirely written by men. Only men can become priests and the Pope is therefore male. In the Bible, Eve is portrayed as being created out of Adam's spare rib.
Islam	The Prophet Muhammad was male. Men make all the legal judgements and are the religious leaders.
Hinduism	Only men can become Brahmin priests. Women cannot approach family shrines when pregnant or menstruating.
Chinese folk religions	Women are associated with Yin and men with Yang spirits, but Yang spirits are more important and powerful.
Orthodox Judaism	Only men can play a full part in religious ceremonies and become rabbis.
Sikhism	The most equal of the major religions since all positions are equally open to men and women. However, in practice, most senior positions are still held by men.

Table 6
Gender inequality in major religions

Feminist perspectives

A variety of feminists have put forward the view that religion is patriarchal.

Key study

Simone de Beauvoir: *The Second Sex*

Simone de Beauvoir (1949) pioneered a feminist view of religion, portraying religion as an instrument of male domination. She argued that men usually control religious organisations and claim that their authority comes from God; for example, kings used to rule by 'Divine Right'. Some religions may portray women as being closer to God, but only if they are passive and do not question male authority. Religion then gives women a false belief that their suffering will be rewarded in heaven. Religion therefore gives women a form of **false consciousness**, which keeps them in their place. It deceives women into thinking they are equal to men, while in reality they are disadvantaged as the 'second sex'.

Essential notes

De Beauvoir is usually considered to be a radical feminist. Her views have similarities with Marxism.

Nawal El Saadawi: The Hidden Face of Eve

Saadawi (1980) is an Egyptian feminist concerned mostly with the oppression of women in the Islamic Arab world. She argues that women are sometimes seriously oppressed in Islamic states. For example, she herself experienced female circumcision, in which part of her clitoris was amputated. Saadawi argues, however, that practices such as female circumcision are not the result of Islam itself but of male misinterpretations of the Qur'an, which distort the true beliefs and are used to justify the exploitation of women.

Evaluation of religion as patriarchal

Some feminist and other sociologists have argued that religion cannot always be seen as patriarchal. For example, Quakerism is one religion that has always had equality between men and women, and inequality within Sikhism is minimal. Furthermore, some religions are becoming less patriarchal. For example:

- Reform Judaism has allowed women to become rabbis since 1972.
- The Church of England now allows the ordination of women and women can also become bishops.

Helen Watson (1994) believes that some religions can be misinterpreted as being patriarchal. For example, she argues that the veiling of women in Islam is not a sign of oppression but a way of protecting women against the male gaze in patriarchal societies where women can be the victims of sexual harassment.

Examiners' notes

These points can provide some evaluation and balance for 18- and 33-mark questions. You can also use other perspectives, which disagree with feminism.

Examiners' notes

A 33-mark question might ask you to discuss the relationship between religion and social change. You will need to include the range of perspectives discussed here and provide a number of examples to support or contradict the various theories.

Religion, social change and the work of Weber

Relationships between religion and social change

The relationship between religion and changes in society can be considered in a number of possible ways.

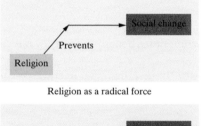

Religion as a conservative force

Religion — Prevents → Social change

Religion as a radical force

Religion — Causes → Social change

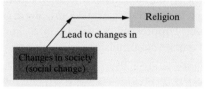

Religion as shaped by society

Changes in society (social change) — Lead to changes in → Religion

Fig. 2
Relationship between religion and changes in society

Examiners' notes

Essay questions on whether religion can be seen as a conservative force or not are quite common. A key point is to show that you understand there can be different meanings to the word 'conservative' in this context.

Religion as a conservative force

The view that religion primarily acts to prevent change is supported by:

- Functionalists, who argue that religion benefits society by promoting stability and integration.
- Marxists, who argue that it benefits the ruling class by helping to promote false class consciousness and thereby retaining ruling-class power (see pp 16–17).
- Most feminists, who argue that it helps to retain patriarchal power (see pp 20–21).

Religion is sometimes seen as a conservative force. Conservative, in this context, can have two meanings:

1. Preventing social change.
2. Preserving traditional values and beliefs.

Usually, these two characteristics go together. For example, successive leaders of the Roman Catholic Church have supported traditional sexual morality that opposes sex outside marriage and abortion. By supporting tradition they have been opposing change.

However, when traditional values have already lost their importance, religion can sometimes be a force for change by supporting traditional values. For example, in Iran in 1979, the Shah, who had Westernised the country and thereby overthrown many traditional Islamic values, was replaced in an Islamic revolution by the Ayatollah Khomeini. Thus religion caused change at the same time as supporting traditional values.

Religion as a radical force

The view that religion can be a **radical force**, that is, a force for change, is supported by:

- **Neo-Marxists** such as Otto Maduro (1982), who points out how Roman Catholic liberation theology in Latin America shows that religion can sometimes become a force for radical change. (See page 19.)
- Max Weber, who argued that religion could be used to support any set of beliefs, including those which lead to changes in society (see pp 24–25).

Religion as shaped by changes in society

This view argues that changes in society largely shape changes in religion. It is supported by:

- Functionalists, who believe that as society evolves it will lead to a change in the role of religion. For example, Comte believed that religion would decline as a result of the increasing importance of **positivist** science. Talcott Parsons believed that religion would lose some of its functions as society developed. He believed it would continue to provide basic **values** (or underpin the value consensus) but it would lose other social functions such as running the education system or directly providing the basis of the legal system.
- Marxists, who believe that changes in religion are shaped by changes in the economic system or **mode of production**. For example, Marxists such as Kautsky thought that the change from Catholicism to Protestantism in some European countries was the result of the change from **feudalism** to **capitalism**. Protestantism was more suited to capitalist societies because of its emphasis on individual relationships with God, whereas Catholicism was more concerned with accepting traditional authority (beliefs that fitted better with feudalism).
- **Postmodernists** believe that the advent of postmodernity has led to significant changes in religion. In particular, they see it as leading to the decline of traditional church-based religions in which believers follow rules laid down by their religion, and the growth of New Age beliefs where people can pick and choose their own belief systems. (This is linked to the decline of **metanarratives** on page 9.)
- The theory of **secularisation** argues that religion has progressively declined in Western societies and has been replaced by **scientific rationalism** where there is little room for faith.

The details of all the above views have been contested by other sociologists, but there is widespread agreement that changes in society can lead to changes in religious beliefs.

Examiners' notes

Some candidates tend to concentrate on religion causing or preventing change. You can provide a fuller answer if you also discuss the effects of social changes on religion where this is relevant.

☞ This topic continues on the next two pages

The Weberian perspective on religion and social change

The most influential sociologist claiming that religion could lead to social change was Max Weber.

Weber (1920) argued against the Marxist view that religion is always shaped by the **economic base** of society. Although he agreed with Marx that religion is sometimes shaped by the economy, he claimed that the relationship can sometimes be reversed so that religion can cause economic change. This was illustrated in his book *The Protestant Ethic and the Spirit of Capitalism*.

Essential notes

Weber founded a whole perspective within sociology, which combines an examination of social action with social structure, and materialism with idealism. By avoiding a one-sided approach, Weber produced a more flexible and less dogmatic perspective than Marxists, functionalists or feminists.

Examiners' notes

These could be useful additional points to make in any answer about Weber.

Key study
Max Weber (1904–5): *The Protestant Ethic and the Spirit of Capitalism*

In this book Weber looked at the reasons for the development of industrial capitalism in Europe and the USA. He argued that at the time many countries, including India and China, had the necessary economic preconditions, including skills, technology and financial systems. However, these countries lacked the necessary beliefs and attitudes for capitalism to emerge. Weber argued that the development of capitalism in Western societies resulted from the right economic conditions plus the existence of a particular set of religious beliefs. He specifically linked the growth of capitalism to the rise of a particular type of Protestantism, Calvinism. This had originated in the 17th century with the ideas of John Calvin. Calvin thought there was a distinct group of the **elect** who were chosen by God, before they were even born, to go to heaven. Those who were not amongst the elect could never get to heaven, however well they behaved. Calvinists who were uncertain about their future fate had to behave virtuously to convince themselves that they were one of the elect and would be going to heaven. This resulted in the Protestant ethic of an **ascetic lifestyle** in which followers chose to forgo life's pleasures such as drinking or dancing. It also encouraged devotion to work, which was seen as God's calling, and the simple lifestyle in which money was not wasted on luxuries. Weber argued that the spirit of capitalism involves a determination to make money, but not to spend it. Instead, money is reinvested in businesses so that they can become ever more profitable. Although this was not the intention of Calvin, Calvinism led to the spirit of capitalism because his followers worked hard and spent little of their money on themselves. Many of the early capitalists were Calvinists, reinvesting their money in their businesses, which grew and became successful. However, capitalism eventually led to the undermining of religious beliefs as it involves the **rational** calculation of profit and loss, and this leaves little room for the faith and devotion necessary in religion. Therefore, Calvinism eventually led to its own downfall because it encouraged secularisation.

Weber has a distinctive theoretical view compared to Marx.

- Karl Marx was a **materialist** – he believed that material forces, such as the economy, shape the development of society.
- Max Weber agreed that material forces were important, but he was also in part an **idealist** – he believed that ideas and beliefs could shape society. For example, in *The Protestant Ethic*, the ideas of Calvinism helped to produce a major economic change, the development of capitalism.

Evaluation of Weber

A number of criticisms have been made of Weber, some of which Weber and his supporters have countered.

Issue in Weber's theory	Argument against Weber	Counter-argument supporting Weber
The nature of Calvinist beliefs	Sombart (1907) argued that Calvinism attacked greed and making money for its own sake.	Weber argued it was not the beliefs but the indirect effects of the belief in predestination that led to the Protestant work ethic.
The reason Calvinists were linked to capitalist businesses	Calvinism was linked to capitalism not because Calvinists believed in predestination, but because, like other non-conformist religions, they were banned from many professions.	Supporters of Weber argue that followers of other non-conformist religions also became successful capitalists, so it was their beliefs that made the difference.
Which came first, capitalism or Protestantism?	The Marxist Kautsky (1953) claimed that capitalism predated and therefore caused Protestantism.	Weber argued that reinvestment and the pursuit of profit, the key features of capitalism, only came after Protestantism.
Where capitalism started	Scotland, Switzerland, Hungary and parts of the Netherlands were strongly Calvinist but were not amongst the first areas to become capitalist.	Marshall (1982) argues that these countries lacked the economic conditions necessary for capitalism to develop.

Table 7
Evaluation of Weber

Examiners' notes

Try to include all these points if you are asked a specific question about Weber, or a couple if you're asked a more general question about religion and social change. Including arguments and counter-arguments demonstrates advanced evaluation skills and is likely to help you get into the top mark band on essay questions.

Whatever the merit of Weber's study of the Protestant ethic, the argument that beliefs can cause change and have an independent effect on society is a broader one, which a number of sociologists support.

Religion, social change and conflict

Examples of religion causing social change

Many sociologists now accept that religion can cause social change.

G. K. Nelson (1986), for example, argues there are many cases where religion has undermined stability or promoted change.

- In the USA in the 1960s the Reverend Martin Luther King and the Southern Christian Leadership Council supported the civil rights movement and this resulted in legislation to reduce racial discrimination.
- The Roman Catholic liberation theology movement in 1979 supported the Sandinistas who took control of Nicaragua.
- In South Africa, Archbishop Tutu was a prominent opponent of apartheid and helped to bring about its end.
- In the 1980s the Roman Catholic Church in Poland joined with the free trade union Solidarity to bring an end to communist control.

More recent examples of religious activity resulting in social change include:

- The 9/11 attacks on the USA by the Islamic organisation Al Qaeda, which resulted in significant changes in the United States foreign policy, including the invasion of Afghanistan, and, to some extent, were used to justify the invasion of Iraq. Both these policies led to regime changes in those countries.
- In Afghanistan, resistance by the Islamic Mujahideen led to the expulsion of occupying forces by the Soviet Union in 1989. This resulted in the Taliban taking control in 1996 and imposing Islamic law before they, in turn, lost control in some parts of the country with the intervention of US forces in response to the 9/11 attacks.

Factors affecting whether or not religion becomes a radical force

It is now widely accepted that religion can cause social change. The question has moved on to in what circumstances religion tends to be conservative (prevents change) and what sometimes leads to religion being a radical force for change.

Meredith B. McGuire (1981) argues that whether religion becomes a force for radical change or not is affected by a range of factors.

- Religions with strong moral codes are more likely to have followers who are critical of society and therefore may take action to change it.
- Societies in which religious beliefs are central to the culture (for example, in Latin America) provide more opportunity for people to use religion to mobilise a movement for change.
- Where religious organisations play a central role in the economic and political structure of society, they have more chance of producing change.

Examiners' notes

Look carefully at the question when choosing which examples to use. If you are asked specifically about contemporary society do not use historical examples. You can also impress the examiner by using very recent examples from the news.

Examiners' notes

More sophisticated conclusions to answers on religion and social change or related topics develop the analysis beyond simply saying religion can sometimes be a radical force.

Religion, conflict and theories

Whether religion can be a force for change or not is closely related to whether it causes **conflict** as, when it does, this can lead to change.

- Functionalism claims that religion tends to prevent conflicts by creating harmony through shared values.
- Marxism and feminism both claim that religion can prevent conflicts by reinforcing the control of dominant groups in society, the ruling class in the case of Marxism and men in the case of feminism.
- Weber recognises that religion can be a cause of conflict as well as harmony.

Other perspectives point out that religion can cause conflict without leading to change.

Examples of religion causing conflict

There are many examples of religion being linked to conflict, e.g. between Protestants and Catholics in Northern Ireland, Muslim Palestinians and Jewish Israelis in the Middle East, Orthodox Serbs, Catholic Croatians and Muslims in Bosnia during the 1990s and Muslims and Hindus in the Indian subcontinent. Some theories have begun to claim that religion causes conflict.

Key study

Samuel Huntington: The clash of civilisations

Samuel Huntington (1993) argues that people see themselves as belonging to **civilisations** that are usually linked to a religion and that therefore religious identities are increasingly important in the modern world. These civilisations are: Western, Confucian (China), Japanese, Islamic, Hindu, Slavic-Orthodox, Latin American and African. When these civilisations come into contact, conflict tends to break out; for example, conflict between Islamic and Western civilisations.

Conflict as caused by non-religious factors

It can often be argued that conflicts apparently based on religion are really about other issues. For example, in Northern Ireland the conflict was more about whether the UK or Eire (Southern Ireland) controlled the North, while in the Middle East the Palestinian-Israeli conflict is about control over land.

Karen Armstrong (2001) argues that the conflict between Islam and the West is not primarily caused by religion but by American foreign policy. The USA has frequently intervened in Muslim countries and often supported regimes that have not brought prosperity to ordinary Muslims.

Steve Bruce (2000) claims that religious factors are often intermingled with non-religious factors in causing conflict. He cites the Palestinian-Israeli conflict where nationality and **ethnicity** are intermingled with religious differences.

Examiners' notes

Questions on the relationship between religion and conflict are quite common, especially as long essay questions. Expand on the view of these briefly summarised theories to develop your answer.

Examiners' notes

Use examples to support or contradict different viewpoints. Look out for other examples of conflict in the media.

Essential notes

Huntington is a controversial social scientist and his ideas have been heavily criticised. There are many examples of supposedly conflicting civilisations living in harmony. Furthermore there is plenty of conflict within civilisations, such as conflict between different types of Christianity (e.g. Protestants and Catholics) or Muslims (e.g. Shia and Sunni Muslims in Iraq).

Examiners' notes

For a sophisticated argument in conclusions on religion and conflict you must point out that much of the apparent conflict between religions could be over other issues.

Fundamentalism

The definition of fundamentalism

Fundamentalist religions are defined by Almond et al. (2003) as a 'pattern of religious militancy by which self-styled true believers attempt to arrest the erosion of religious identity … and create viable alternatives to secular institutions and behaviour'.

In other words, fundamentalist religions believe that a set of religious beliefs has been watered down or is under threat. They are opposed to the decline of those beliefs and wish to return to the original, basic, or 'fundamental' beliefs of their religion.

Fundamentalists often return to the beliefs of an original text on which their religion is based, claiming that other followers have strayed away from the original teachings and compromise the integrity of their religion. Fundamentalism is often seen as a response to a general decline of the influence of religion in the world, or **secularisation.**

Fundamentalism, conflict and social change

Fundamentalism causes conflict with other groups who they see as a threat to their religion. It is also likely to cause conflict with other followers of the same religion who do not share the interpretation of fundamentalists.

Fundamentalism can be seen as a response to changes, since fundamentalists seek to reverse changes that have already taken place in society or religion. It therefore tends to be a **conservative force** in terms of preserving traditional values but a **radical force** in terms of seeking social change.

Examples of fundamentalism

Fundamentalism has appeared in a wide variety of religions in a wide variety of contexts and appears to be becoming more common in the modern world.

Examples include:

- The New Christian Right, a Protestant fundamentalist group in the USA. They are radical Christians with a large following supporting a literal interpretation of the Bible.
- Al Qaeda, a Muslim group led by Osama bin Laden, originating in Saudi Arabia/Afghanistan but with a worldwide following. They are responsible for terrorist attacks including the 9/11 attacks on the USA.
- Hamas, a group of Palestinian Muslim fundamentalists. They were elected to power in the Gaza Strip and are opposed to Israeli occupation of Palestinian territories. They have fought wars with Israel and sponsored terrorist tactics.
- Bharatiya Janata Party (BJP), a Hindu fundamentalist group in India. They believe India should be run along Hindu religious lines rather than secular lines, recognising all religious minorities.

Examiners' notes

Fundamentalism could appear in a question in its own, in conjunction with another issue, such as secularisation or social change, or can be used in an answer to a range of other questions that do not specifically mention it.

Examiners' notes

These arguments can be used to evaluate theories: fundamentalism integrates believers (as functionalists would argue) and it may appeal to the disadvantaged and oppressed (as Marxists claim). But it often acts as a radical force, so it also contradicts those theories.

Examiners' notes

These examples are useful evidence for questions on fundamentalism and also on religion and conflict, and religion and change.

Fundamentalism and secularisation

Steve Bruce (2000) believes that fundamentalism is caused by secularisation. He argues that the decline of religion, and **modernisation** in which science and **rationality** are favoured, tend to undermine traditional religious faith.

In addition, fundamentalism is more likely to develop when:

- religion has a single sacred text over which followers can argue
- a religion lacks centralised authoritarian control, without which it is easier for alternative interpretations of the religion to develop
- followers have a common enemy, for example, in the case of Muslim fundamentalism, the United States and Israel
- there is a ready supply of potential recruits; for example, Hamas can draw on the large numbers of impoverished, unemployed young men in Palestine
- there is little opportunity to express grievances through legitimate politics, in which case fundamentalism tends to become more radical; for example, in Iran before 1979 the Western-backed Shah was a dictator imposing modernisation on the country – he was opposed by Muslim fundamentalists and overthrown in the revolution.

In many parts of the world fundamentalism may represent a deliberate rejection of Western modernisation due to resentment of its effects.

Key study

Almond, Scott, Appleby and Sivan: The causes of fundamentalism

Almond et al. (2003) agree secularisation and modernisation helped to produce fundamentalism but in addition they see it as being caused by:

- low levels of education and high levels of inequality
- the displacement of people by war
- economic problems
- chance events such as poor harvests
- Western imperialism; fundamentalist beliefs can develop amongst those opposed to US involvement in a region
- effective leadership necessary to mobilise those with a grievance.

Karen Armstrong: Islam and the West

Karen Armstrong (2001) argues that there is nothing in the Islamic religion, which tends to lead towards fundamentalist beliefs. For more than a century, most Islamic leaders were in favour of Westernisation and modernisation. However, the attempts to impose modernisation too rapidly on Islamic countries without concern for the welfare of the poor has built up resentments within many Islamic populations in the world. This has led to the growth of Islamic fundamentalism.

Essential notes

Fundamentalism seems to contradict the theory of secularisation. Thirty or 40 years ago few commentators or sociologists expected an upsurge in fundamentalist religious beliefs around the world.

Essential notes

Armstrong shows that economic and political factors can often lie behind changes that appear to be caused largely or entirely by developments within religion.

Churches, denominations and sects

Typologies of religious organisation

Although individuals can have their own religious beliefs without belonging to an organisation, most believers are members of religious organisations, which tend to shape their practices and beliefs.

In 1931 Ernst Troeltsch defined the difference between a **church** and a **sect**. Prior to this, in 1929, H. R. Niebuhr had argued that to take account of the situation in the United States an intermediate type of religious organisation, the **denomination**, had to be distinguished from churches and sects.

The church

According to Troeltsch (1931) the church is a large religious organisation where members do not usually have to demonstrate their faith; instead they are born into it and recruited before they can understand its teachings.

Churches attempt to be universal, that is, include all members of a society. Because of their size, members are drawn from all classes, but since the church is part of the establishment, higher classes are particularly well represented. Partly for this reason, churches tend to be ideologically conservative, supporting the **values** and beliefs of those in a position of **power** in society.

Churches are usually tied to the **state**; for example, the Roman Catholic Church throughout the Middle Ages in most of Europe. In Britain today, the Church of England is still connected to the state since the Queen is head of both the Church of England and the state.

Churches often carry out important social **functions**, such as being involved in politics and running schools. Members of churches continue to carry out normal social roles and the demands on individuals to demonstrate their faith are not usually very great in terms of restriction on their behaviour. Churches are formal organisations with a **hierarchy** of paid officials and may be quite rich; in particular, they often own extensive holdings of land.

Churches traditionally try to protect and preserve a monopoly of the religious truth, claiming they are the only genuine religion within a society.

Evaluation of the definition of a church

Steve Bruce (1996) believes that the above definition of churches was appropriate in pre-modern Christian societies. However, he points out that in 1517 Martin Luther began to question the teachings of the medieval church, and since then there have been competing Christian institutions, which have led to **religious pluralism**.

There are a number of organisations today, which are generally seen as churches but do not conform to Troeltsch's definition.

- Many churches do not have a majority of the population as active members. For example, in 2005 only 870 000 people were active members of the Church of England or other Anglican churches.

- Churches are not always connected to the state and can even be opposed to it, such as supporters of Roman Catholic **liberation theology** in parts of Latin America.
- Churches are not always ideologically conservative. Grace Davie (1989) claims there are growing numbers of radical bishops in the Church of England.
- Most churches do not claim a monopoly of the religious truth but tolerate the existence of other religions. The ecumenical movement encourages cooperation amongst the different Christian churches.

Denominations

Troeltsch based his definition of a church on Europe, but in the United States there has never been a single established church. The American sociologist Niebuhr (1929) argued that a different type of religious organisation, the denomination, needed to be distinguished.

In many respects denominations are similar to churches – they are formal organisations with a hierarchy of officials and it is not difficult to become a member. They draw members from all parts of society, but compared to churches have more supporters from working-class and lower middle-class backgrounds.

Denominations tend to be conservative, generally accepting the norms and values of society, though they may have slightly different values from others. For example, Methodists are discouraged from drinking and gambling (although there are no absolute restrictions and those who take part in these activities are likely to be subject to no more than mild disapproval).

Unlike churches, denominations are not connected to a state. Although they are not universal, a denomination reflects the religion of a significant minority. In 2006, for example, 287 600 people attended Methodist churches in England.

They do not claim a monopoly of the religious truth, as they have to coexist with other religious organisations.

Sects

According to Troeltsch, sects are essentially the polar opposite of churches.

They are much smaller organisations. The larger ones tend to have thousands of members rather than millions, while some have only a handful of members.

They are not connected to the state and tend to have **norms** and values that are quite different from those of the wider society, so they can be regarded with suspicion and hostility by non-members. They may even be in opposition to the state and clash with the law; they tend to be **radical** rather than conservative.

Sect members often withdraw from the wider world and dedicate their lives to the sect. For example, sect members may live in a commune. Members are also expected to show deep commitment to the organisation and usually have to adhere to a strict morality imposed on them.

Examiners' notes

Sects such as this are clear examples of religion being a radical force. They might not have much influence on the wider society but they are in favour of changes, and this can lead to conflict.

☞ **This topic continues on the next two pages**

Sects tend only to recruit adults who are willing and able to demonstrate their commitment to the sect. Children are not usually admitted until they are old enough to demonstrate this commitment. The sect exercises a much stronger control over members than churches or denominations.

Unlike denominations, sects do not tolerate alternative religious views but claim a monopoly of the religious truth.

Usually, sects are not organised through a bureaucratic structure and hierarchy, but are led by a single **charismatic leader** whose personality helps to keep the sect together.

Key study
David Koresh and the Branch Davidians

In the 1990s David Koresh took over a sect in Waco, Texas. He told his followers that he was David the Lamb from the Bible and that the apocalyptic end of the earth was imminent. He demanded absolute loyalty from his members, for example, requiring the men to allow him to have sex with their wives and daughters if he chose to. The sect stockpiled weapons and when the Bureau of Alcohol, Tobacco and Firearms (BATF) tried to raid the compound, they were met with armed resistance. Four of the BATF agents and several Davidians were killed and a prolonged siege with the FBI resulted. After 51 days, an attempt to end the siege led to a fire in which almost 80 Branch Davidians were killed.

The main characteristics of the three types of religious organisation are summarised in table 8.

Table 8
The main characteristics of churches, denominations and sects

	Church	Denomination	Sect
Sociologist identifying these factors	Troeltsch (1931)	Niebuhr (1929)	Troeltsch (1931)
Example	Roman Catholic Church	Methodists	Jehovah's Witnesses
Social background of members	Members drawn from all classes in society, although upper class particularly likely to join	No universal appeal, not connected with the upper class	Connected with the lower classes
Relationship to state	Sometimes closely connected to the state	Does not identify with the state, approves of the separation of church and state	Often in opposition to the state

	Church	Denomination	Sect
Relationship to society	Churches accept and affirm life in this world	Members generally accept the norms and values of society	Members tend to reject the values of the world that surrounds them
Demands on members	Members do not have to demonstrate their faith to belong to a church	Some minor restrictions may be placed on members (e.g. Methodists are discouraged from drinking and gambling)	Deep commitment demanded from members; they may be expected to withdraw from life outside the sect
Tolerance	Will often jealously guard their monopoly of religious truth	Does not claim a monopoly of religious truth and is tolerant of other religions	Tend to believe that they possess a monopoly of religious truth
Type of organisation	A formal organisation with a hierarchy of paid officials	Usually smaller than a church but still a formal organisation with a hierarchy of paid officials	Authority often rests with a charismatic leader whose special qualities persuade others to follow him

Evaluation of traditional religious typology

Steve Bruce (1995) argues that both churches and sects have drifted towards the characteristics of a denomination. Churches can no longer claim a monopoly on religious truth and are no longer universal; they are therefore increasingly like denominations. Furthermore, groups such as Jehovah's Witnesses and Pentecostals, which used to be regarded as sects, now tend to be seen as denominations.

Alan Aldridge (2000) argues that groups such as the Church of the Latter Day Saints (Mormons) have an ambiguous position. In the USA, they are seen as just one amongst many denominations, but in the UK they are viewed as more deviant and therefore regarded more like a sect.

Introduction of the cult

The definition of sect worked well in earlier decades of the 20th century. However, by the 1960s and 1970s a wider variety of alternative religious groups had sprung up in the USA and Europe. This meant that the typology of church, denomination and sect did not work so well. As a result, a fourth type of organisation, the **cult**, is now sometimes distinguished and alternative ways of classifying these **new religious movements** have been devised.

Cults, sects and new religious movements

Cults

In everyday usage, the term cult is often used interchangeably with the term sect. However, sociologists distinguish between sects and cults as two different types of organisation. Like sects, cults are more individualistic than other religious organisations and tend to be relatively small groups, although some can have widespread support. However, in general terms, the definition of a cult differs from a sect in that:

- Their belief systems do not usually involve a belief in God or gods. They tolerate and accept the existence of other belief systems.
- Many lack clear rules about how they believe their supporters should behave.
- Rather than having 'believers', they tend to have 'customers' who buy the services of the organisation but are not required to have great commitment to it.

Steve Bruce (1995) defines a cult as a 'loosely knit group organised around some common themes and interests, lacking any sharply defined and exclusive belief system'.

An alternative definition of cults is offered by Stark and Bainbridge (1985), who describe them as any organisation that has beliefs that are novel for a particular society. Cults have not broken away from an existing religion (as sects often have) but have either devised a completely new set of beliefs or imported beliefs or religious tradition from outside that society. For example, some cults have based their ideas upon science fiction or Freudian psychology. Others have imported ideas from Eastern religions, such as Buddhism, into Western societies.

Wallis' definition of religious organisations

Another way of defining a cult was provided by Roy Wallis (1976) in his general **typology** of all religious organisations. He distinguishes organisations according to whether they are:

- **Respectable** (they are seen as conforming to the main norms and values of society) or **deviant** (they are not seen as conforming to the norms and values of society).
- **Uniquely legitimate** (they believe they have the only true religion and no other beliefs should be accepted) or **pluralistically legitimate** (they accept the right of other belief systems to exist).

The four types of religious organisation defined by this categorisation are shown in table 9.

Table 9
Wallis' typology of religious organisations

	Respectable	Deviant
Uniquely legitimate	Church	Sect
Pluralistically legitimate	Denomination	Cult

New religious movements

In the 1970s there was a rapid growth of smaller religious organisations. Roy Wallis (1984) described these organisations as new religious movements.

He distinguishes between three types of new religious movement.

1. World-rejecting new religious movements
2. World-affirming new religious movements
3. World-accommodating new religious movements

1. World-rejecting new religious movements

World-rejecting new religious movements have the most in common with sects. Their beliefs are very critical of the outside world and therefore they often seek radical change.

- To achieve salvation, members are expected to make a sharp break with conventional life when they join the movement. The organisations often act as **total institutions**, which control every aspect of the lives of their members.
- Members are expected to be highly disciplined and usually submit to the rigours of an **ascetic lifestyle** (they devote themselves to their religion rather than to personal pleasure).
- They have a reputation for brainwashing members. Family and friends are cut off and are often unable to understand the reasons for joining the movement.
- Most world-rejecting new religious movements base their lives around a **commune**.
- Examples include Peoples Temple, Branch Davidians and the Children of God.

Key study
Peoples Temple

Set up in 1955 by the Reverend Jim Jones, this group recruited both affluent white followers and black ghetto dwellers from Northern California. It had a radical ideology based upon a combination of religion and **Marxism**. The sect was strictly controlled by the charismatic leader who claimed to be able to perform miracle medical cures. Under investigation from the US authorities, Jones moved the sect to the rainforests of Guyana where members withdrew from the outside world. In 1978 the sect was again being investigated, and a US congressman and several journalists were killed. Fearing the consequences, the members agreed to commit mass suicide and the entire sect of over 900 people died through poisoning – most committed suicide, although some appeared to have been injected.

2. World-affirming new religious movements

World-affirming new religious movements often lack the typical characteristics of a religion. For example, some do not involve a belief in God.

- Rather than turning against the world, these movements are positive about the world but argue that individuals are often lacking something spiritually and this is preventing them from achieving fulfilment and success.

Examiners' notes

This organisation is a good example of a radical sect and so is relevant to questions on social change and conservativism.

Essential notes

World-affirming new religious movements have probably been the most influential of the three types and certainly have the most followers. They are also often connected to New Age beliefs (see pp 42–43).

☞ This topic continues on the next two pages

- They offer their followers access to supernatural or spiritual powers that will enhance their ability to live fulfilling and successful lives.
- Followers are unlikely to live in a commune, or give up other aspects of their lives. Usually, they simply practise some life-affirming activity in order to make themselves more successful. However, there is sometimes a hard-core of followers who do give up their normal lives to follow the movement.
- Examples of these movements include Transcendental Meditation (TM), Erhard Seminars Training (EST) and Scientology.

Key study
Transcendental Meditation (TM)

TM is based upon the Hindu religion and was first introduced into the West in the late 1950s by the Maharishi Mahesh Yogi who for a while was followed by the Beatles. It teaches a meditational technique in which followers are given an individual mantra on which they concentrate for some 20 minutes twice a day. It is claimed that this technique can provide 'unbounded awareness', with beneficial effects for the individual and for society. Most followers pay for a few sessions to learn the technique and then practise at home, but there are a few committed followers who base their lives around TM.

3. World-accommodating new religious movements

These are often offshoots of an existing major church or denomination.

- Typically, they neither accept nor reject the world as it is, they simply live with it.
- They are concerned more with religious rather than worldly questions.
- Such groups seek to restore spiritual purity to a religion that they believe has lost its commitment to its core values.
- Examples include Subud and Neo-Pentecostalism.

Examiners' notes

Examples of new religious movements such as this, which tend to attract members from minority ethnic groups, can be used in discussions of social groups and participation in organised religion.

Key study
Neo-Pentecostalism

This is a Christian group, which argues that the original teachings of the Bible have been watered down. In particular, the importance of the Holy Spirit has been neglected by other versions of Christianity. Neo-Pentecostalists believe that the Holy Spirit can speak directly through the bodies of humans. They therefore engage in the practice of 'speaking in tongues' when they feel possessed by the spirit who communicates through their mouths. Although they have radical religious views, neo-Pentecostalists are otherwise conforming members of society. The group appeals particularly to Black-African and African-Caribbean populations in the UK and USA.

The middle ground

Wallis accepts that some organisations do not fit neatly into his typology, e.g. their members might live in communes but still go out and hold conventional jobs. An example is the Healthy, Happy, Holy Organisation (3HO), based partly upon the Sikh religion, where followers live in communes or ashrams but work outside the sect as well. Other examples are Meher Baba and the Divine Light Mission.

Criticisms of Wallis

Beckford (1985) argues that the categories in Wallis' scheme are hard to apply because it is not clear whether the teaching of the movement or the beliefs of individual members are more important.

He also argues that Wallis does not take account of the diversity of views that often exist within a single organisation.

Stark and Bainbridge: Categorising religions

Stark and Bainbridge (1985) are critical of all typologies, arguing that there are always overlaps between categories. Instead, they rank organisations in terms of their degree of tension with society, ranging from churches at one end to cults at the other extreme. However, they then go on to classify the smaller types of religious organisation into their own typology.

1. Sects are small religious groups, which are an offshoot of an existing religion and are in a high degree of tension with the outside world.
2. Cults are small religious groups, which are either novel or based upon a religion from another society. They can be divided into three types.
    - **Audience cults**. These require little commitment from their followers and often act as little more than a form of entertainment. Examples include astrology.
    - **Client cults**. These offer services to their followers, who are seen as customers. They offer a way of enhancing life rather than an alternative lifestyle. Examples are Scientology and Transcendental Meditation (TM).
    - **Cult movements**. Members may expect to give up aspects of their life by, for example, living in a commune. They offer members a complete spiritual package including answers to core questions such as what happens after death. An example is the Heaven's Gate cult.

Criticisms of Stark and Bainbridge

A problem with Stark and Bainbridge's definitions is that they argue that typologies do not adequately categorise religions because the boundaries are not clear-cut, but then produce their own typology, which could be criticised for the same reason, e.g. it is unclear how much involvement members have to have for an organisation to be regarded as a cult movement rather than a client cult.

Examiners' notes

Remember to include these types of criticism in essay questions to get into the higher bands for analytical and evaluative skills.

Examiners' notes

This is an alternative to the other typologies and very useful for developing essays on this topic.

Examiners' notes

This topic could be used for an 18-mark question or linked to other topics (such as secularisation or the future of sects) for a longer essay.

Table 10
New religious movements: UK membership and groups, 1995–2005

The growth of sects and cults

Religious sects and cults have existed for centuries, but most current sects and cults originated in the 20th century. Many of these new organisations appeared in the 1960s and 1970s.

Table 10 demonstrates the growth of new religious movements since 1995.

Date	Members	No. of new groups
1995	14 350	No figures available
2000	29 503	775
2005	37 412	829

Between 1995 and 2005, the number of Scientologists grew from 121 800 to 165 000 and the number of Unificationists ('Moonies') more than trebled to 1 200. Note, however, that the reliability of these figures is open to question. For example, Scientologists class anyone who has completed a Scientology course as a member.

In addition to the numbers in the table, there are also many nontrinitarian groups, which are sometimes regarded as new religious movements. There were 547 000 members of such groups in 2005.

Marginality

Max Weber (1922) argued that sects tended to develop amongst **marginal** groups in society, that is, people outside the mainstream of social life who felt that they were not receiving the **status** and economic rewards they deserved. These sects tended to develop a **theodicy of disprivilege** – a religious explanation and justification for their disadvantage, often promising them salvation in the afterlife.

Brian Wilson (1970) argues that situations such as defeat in war, natural disaster and economic collapse could lead to groups becoming marginalised and turning to new religions.

Some of those recruited to new religious movements in the 1960s were from disadvantaged backgrounds; for example, the Black Muslims largely recruited very poor black Americans.

Although most of the members of **world-rejecting new religious movements** were drawn from young, white, middle-class Americans and Europeans, Wallis argues that despite their backgrounds many of these recruits were marginal to society; they were often drug users, hippies, drop-outs or surfers.

Relative deprivation

The sense of marginalisation experienced by young, middle-class Americans can be explained through the concept of **relative deprivation**. This refers to people experiencing a sense of deprivation (or lacking something) even if they are not poor economically.

Wallis believes that in the 1960s a significant number of young people felt spiritually deprived in a world they saw as too materialistic and impersonal. Sects and cults offered them an opportunity to regain a sense of spiritual wholeness.

Essential notes

Arguments about marginality and relative deprivation link to the Marxist view that religion is a response to disadvantage and oppression, but develop this viewpoint by showing that disadvantage can be relative rather than absolute.

Social change

Brian Wilson (1970) argues that sects arise during periods of rapid social change when traditional norms are disrupted, and social relationships come to lack consistent meaning.

An early example of this is the Methodist movement, which started off as a sect. This movement could be seen as a response of the urban working class to the chaos and uncertainty of life in the new industrial towns and cities. It offered support to those trying to make sense of, and survive in, the new, hostile environment.

Steve Bruce (1996) sees the development of sects and cults as a reaction to **modernisation** and **secularisation**. As conventional institutional religion has lost its influence, people have turned to alternatives.

More recently, as people have lost strong beliefs and commitments, cults have become popular because they generally require fewer sacrifices and little religious observance.

The growth of new religious movements

Roy Wallis (1984) gave specific reasons for the development of new religious movements in the 1960s. These were:

1. The growth of higher education, which created an extended period of transition between childhood and adulthood. This left young people with a period of freedom in which they could experiment, since they had few responsibilities.
2. A belief that new technology would lead to an end to both scarcity and the need for commitment to hard work.
3. The growth of radical political movements, which provided an alternative to dominant social norms and values.

New religious movements offer the possibility of a more spiritual and caring way of life.

Bruce (1995) argues that in the 1970s the hippie culture and counter-culture had failed to change the world and by the end of this decade some young people were becoming disillusioned with the movements. Consequently, they sought another path to salvation, through religion rather than through peace and love.

World-affirming new religious movements tend to appeal to those aspiring to be successful while still seeking a spiritual side to their lives.

Bruce (1996) believes that world-affirming new religious movements are largely a response to the **rationalisation** of the modern world, in which organisations and people are primarily concerned with achieving specific objectives rather than achieving a sense of fulfilment. Modern life is **fragmented** and people may have little sense of **identity**. World-affirming movements can fill this gap.

Middle-ground groups developed more from the mid-1970s as economic recession began to bite following a long period of prosperity. Wallis (1984) argues that these groups appealed mainly to former drop-outs who sought a path back towards participation in society.

Examiners' notes

Use this material for questions on religion and social change as it shows how changes in society can lead to changes in religion.

Essential notes

Whether the development of new religious movements can be seen as evidence for, or against, secularisation has been hotly debated. More details of this dispute can be found on pp 54–55.

The development of sects

Sects as short-lived organisations

H. R. Niebuhr (1929) argued that sects could not survive more than a single generation without changing or disappearing.

The reasons for this were:

1. Sect membership is based upon voluntary adult commitment where people choose to follow the beliefs of the religion. Once members start to have children, the children themselves cannot give the same commitment because they are not old enough to understand the teachings of the sect. Because of this, they will not have the same fervour as the first generation, the organisation will become less extreme and will turn into a denomination.

2. Sects that depend upon a charismatic leader will tend to disappear when that leader dies. Alternatively, following the death, the organisation might develop a **bureaucratic** structure rather than being held together by the charisma of an individual. It will therefore tend to become a denomination.

3. Niebuhr believed that the ideology of many sects contains the seeds of its own destruction. Sects with an ascetic creed will encourage their members to work hard and save money. As a result, the members will be upwardly socially mobile and will no longer want to belong to an organisation that caters for marginal members of society. Once again, the sect would change to accommodate this by becoming a denomination, or it would disappear as members left.

Niebuhr's ideas can be illustrated by the example of the Methodists. They were originally a radical group opposed to conventional religions, with members who were marginal in society. However, as the membership rose in status, it became a denomination and its rejection of society was watered down.

Another reason why sects or cults may disappear is because of the death of its members through mass suicide, murder or confrontation with the authorities. Examples include:

- The Peoples Temple cult, who were all poisoned in the jungles of Guyana. (See page 35.)
- The Heaven's Gate cult, who all committed mass suicide.
- The Branch Davidians, many of whom died in a fire following a violent confrontation with the US authorities. (See page 32.)

The life-cycle of sects

Brian Wilson (1966) rejected Niebuhr's thesis that all sects would be short-lived. He pointed out that some sects do survive for long periods of time and argued that the key factor influencing the future of sects was their belief about how they would be saved.

He identified two types of sects:

Examiners' notes

Look carefully at the wording of any question relating to why members of sects may not remain in them for a long time. You may need to explain why individuals leave rather than why the organisation as a whole does not last long.

Examiners' notes

In questions linking different issues (for example, changes in support for the different types of religious institution), select very carefully the material that is relevant.

Examiners' notes

In longer questions on this topic, Wilson's ideas allow you to develop some evaluation and analysis so that you can get into higher mark bands.

Type of sect	Beliefs	Consequences of beliefs
Conversionist/ evangelical sects	Attempt to convert as many people as possible to their religious beliefs	Likely to expand and become a denomination
Adventist sects	Believe that God will return to judge people and only sect members will gain a place in heaven	Membership restricted and therefore likely to remain an exclusive sect (e.g. Jehovah's Witnesses and Seventh Day Adventists)

Table 11
Brian Wilson: Sect ideology and survival

More recently, Wilson (2003) has argued that sects that survive a long time, including Quakers and Pentecostalists, have succeeded in recruiting the children of followers and integrating them into the sect. This has helped to keep the sect isolated from secular influences in society at large.

However, eventually, rising educational standards, increased opportunities and, with new media and globalisation, the difficulties of isolating the sect from wider society may threaten the ability of sects to survive as highly religious organisations.

Internal ideology and the wider society

Wallis (1984) takes a more complex view, arguing that the future of sects depends both on internal ideology and external circumstances.

1. World-rejecting sects often change their stance as time passes. For example, in the 1970s, economic recession discouraged individuals from dropping out of society and groups such as the Children of God softened their hostility to society. Wallis notes that groups may also be destroyed by the actions of their charismatic leader but points out that as new groups in society become marginal, new sects develop. This type of organisation is unstable, but a few do survive long term, for example, the Unificationists.
2. World-affirming movements often sell their services as a commodity, so just like businesses they can suffer from a lack of customers and competition in the market-place. However, the groups will not necessarily disappear – some will change to another type of organisation. For example, in the 1970s, Transcendental Meditation grew even more world-affirming in order to broaden its appeal. These types of groups are very flexible and can evolve as circumstances change.
3. **World-accommodating** movements tend to be the most stable type of new religious movement, continuing for long periods without major changes.
4. Movements of the middle-ground tend to be very unstable and are likely to shift between being world-rejecting and world-affirming, depending on the needs and wishes of the membership. This can lead to splits within the movement; for example, the Process Church split into two factions in 1973.

Essential notes

Stark and Bainbridge (1985) have an alternative view. They believe that many sects are short-lived but as these are constantly being replaced by new ones there is a frequent turnover both in membership and in organisations.

The New Age

Definition and examples

The term the **New Age** became prominent in the 1980s. However, beliefs similar to what is now called the New Age were present in earlier decades in some new religious movements and cults.

In a general sense, the New Age refers to sets of beliefs and activities, which contain a spiritual element but are not organised in the same way as traditional **religion.** Often New Age beliefs exist independent of any organisations and spread through aspects of culture such as films, music, books, shops and seminars.

Paul Heelas et al. (2000) describes the environment in which the New Age exists as the **holistic milieu**. Unlike the **congregational domain**, where people meet regularly for collective worship, the holistic milieu involves more one-to-one activities (for example, between a healer and a client) and small group activities (for example, yoga classes).

Examples of New Age beliefs include:

- clairvoyance
- paganism, witchcraft or magic
- spirit guides or spirit masters
- Feng shui
- the Findhorn community in Scotland (which grows vegetables with the help of plant spirits)
- Scientology
- aliens making contact with humans
- various forms of alternative medicine, including self-healing, herbal remedies, aromatherapy and reflexology.

Themes of the New Age

New Age beliefs are extremely diverse, but Paul Heelas (1996) identifies two main themes that run through all varieties of the New Age.

Theme	Explanation of theme
Self-spirituality	Instead of looking to a traditional religion, look inside yourself for a sense of spirituality. Rather than worshipping external gods, attempt to perfect yourself and discover your own, hidden spiritual depths.
Detraditionalisation	A rejection of traditional sources of authority such as churches and conventional moral or ethical values. You are responsible for your own actions and for discovering your own truth, through getting in touch with your spirituality.

Table 12
The themes of the New Age

Despite the existence of these common themes, according to Heelas, there are variations within the New Age.

Type of New Age belief	Emphasis
World-affirming, with an emphasis on the outer world	Focus on the practical usefulness of the New Age for achieving objectives (e.g. practising Transcendental Meditation to help you succeed in your career).
World-rejecting, with an emphasis on the inner world of the individual	Focus upon turning away from the world and worldly success, towards inner reflection (e.g. Buddhist meditation).
Best of both worlds with both an inner and an outer emphasis	Combines a desire for spiritual satisfaction and worldly success. Most aspects of the New Age (e.g. spiritual healing) combine the two.

Examiners' notes

Use this to develop more sophisticated discussions of the complexity of the New Age. It can also highlight the difficulties in defining religion.

Table 13
Variations in the New Age

Reasons for the growth of the New Age

Postmodernists such as John Drane (1999) see the growth of the New Age as a response to the failure of the emphasis on **science** and material success in **modernity**. The Enlightenment beliefs of the 17th and 18th centuries claimed that science and **rationality** could solve the world's problems. However, events such as global warming have shown that harm can be done in the name of progress. As a result, New Agers are turning away from science, to an era of **postmodernity** where they look for inner spiritual satisfaction.

Steve Bruce (1995) does not believe we have moved to an era of postmodernity but sees the New Age as a product of modernity. Modernity emphasises **individualism** and he sees the New Age as an extreme version of individualism. The New Age is closely linked to the **human potential movement** in which people believe that through self-improvement they can achieve perfection, and in doing so improve the world about them. The New Age particularly appeals to people such as journalists, actors, writers and counsellors. These generally university-educated middle classes have experienced personal development and believe this is the way to achieve progress. The New Age is also a symptom of the relativism of knowledge in an individualistic society; truth depends upon your personal viewpoint rather than an **objective** truth.

Paul Heelas (1996) also sees the New Age as a product of modernity. He argues that four aspects of modernity give rise to the New Age.

1. People have a multiplicity of roles so they lose a sense of their true self. The New Age helps to restore this.
2. **Consumer culture** encourages people to attain perfection through what they buy. The attempt to achieve spiritual perfection is an extension of this.
3. In a rapidly changing society, when traditional norms and values are being disrupted, people use spiritual beliefs to avoid insecurity.
4. The decline of traditional religion such as Christianity leaves a spiritual gap, which is partly filled by the New Age.

Heelas claims that the New Age is part of a **spiritual revolution**, involving a shift towards subjective life and away from traditional religions.

Essential notes

For Drane, the growth of the New Age is an important development that contradicts the theory of secularisation. Bruce, on the other hand, believes that it is not very significant spiritually and has weak effects on people's beliefs and behaviour compared to more traditional religions.

Essential notes

The idea of a spiritual revolution implies that one type of spirituality is replacing another; spiritual beliefs remain important but the nature of those beliefs has changed. These issues are discussed in more detail in the sections on secularisation.

Social class, age and religious participation
Social class and religious participation
Marxist theories of class and religious participation

According to **Marxists**, **social class** is closely related to religious participation. They believe that society is divided between two classes.

1. The **ruling class**, who own the **means of production** (such as land, capital, raw materials and machinery).
2. The **subject class**, who have to work for the ruling class. In slave societies, the workers are owned by the ruling class.

Karl Marx (1844) described religion in **capitalist societies** as the 'opium of the masses'. He saw it as acting like a drug by giving its followers a false sense of well-being and distorting reality. Marx believed that religion started in the subject classes as a way of coping with oppression, but it was later adopted by the ruling classes as a way of justifying their advantaged position in society. Marx therefore believed that all classes believed in religion, although for slightly different reasons.

Neo-Marxists such as Otto Maduro (1982) argue that where religious movements become a radical force for change they can become dominated by the subject class. For example, the **liberation theology** movement amongst Catholics in Latin America was largely supported by the poor who wanted to use religion to improve their position in society.

Social class and types of religious organisation

Although there are no reliable figures on the participation of different social classes in each type of religious organisation, a variety of theorists have suggested that there are links between social class and different types of religious organisations.

- **Churches:** aspire to include members from all classes. However, in contemporary Britain, the upper class and upper middle class are overrepresented because of an association with the establishment and a generally **conservative ideology**.
- **Denominations:** slightly anti-establishment as they have broken away from the religious mainstream. However, Wallis (1984) notes that they are respectable organisations and therefore tend not to attract the lowest classes. Appeal most to the upper working class and the lower middle class.
- **Sects:** traditionally have recruited the most disadvantaged members of society. Require members to give up their previous life, so those with much to lose are unlikely to join. However, it can give the deprived a way of coping with their disadvantages. The Black Muslims in the USA, for example, tend to recruit the most disadvantaged black Americans. Wallis argues that in the 1960s and 1970s they also began to appeal to the 'relatively deprived' middle class of affluent students who were seeking to compensate for their lack of a spiritual life.
- **Cults: client cults** (as classified by Stark and Bainbridge, 1985) or **world-affirming new religious movements** (Wallis' term) appeal

to the already successful and affluent who want to become more successful. Other cult movements are similar to sects and tend to attract the disadvantaged or relatively deprived.

- The **New Age:** according to Paul Heelas (1996) the New Age tends to appeal to the middle class (and particularly women). Steve Bruce (2002) believes that it appeals to those in expressive professions such as the media, teaching and counselling because they believe in self-improvement and the New Age is linked to the **human potential movement**.

Age and religious participation

Research evidence clearly shows that in the UK, older people are more likely to go to church. According to Brierley (2005), in 1979 the average age of the church-goer was 37 but by 2005 it was 49. In 2005, nearly 60% of churches had nobody attending between the ages of 15 and 19. Heelas et al. (2005) also found that most of those involved with the New Age movement are middle-aged or older.

Reasons for age differences in participation

David Voas and Alasdair Crockett (2005) identify three possible explanations for the preponderance of older people participating in religion.

It could be the result of people becoming more religious as they age. This could be because of life experiences, such as having children (they may think it is important to **socialise** their children into religious beliefs and therefore return to religious observance themselves), or because of getting closer to death.

There could be a **period effect** where those born in a particular period (a **cohort**) are more likely to be religious than those born at another time.

The progressive decline of religion (**secularisation**) could mean that each generation is less religious than the previous one.

Using the British Social Attitudes Survey, Voas and Crockett found no evidence that people became progressively more religious over time, or that specific cohorts were becoming less religious. They concluded that secularisation was making each generation less religious than the previous one. There was a progressive decline, partly because each generation was less inclined to socialise their children into religious belief than the previous generation.

Heelas et al. (2005) believe that New Age beliefs in the **holistic milieu** are growing rapidly despite few young people being involved with it (see page 43).

Examiners' notes

If you discuss this issue it is essential that you can explain that these three possible causes could all be reasons for the clear-cut relationship between older age groups and greater religiosity.

Gender and religious participation

Evidence of gender differences in religious participation

There is a range of evidence that women tend to be more likely to participate in religion than men.

The Church Census records participation in churches and denominations in England and Wales. Table 14 shows that between 1979 and 2005, women were consistently more likely to attend.

Date	Attenders who were male	Attenders who were female
1979	45%	55%
1989	42%	58%
2005	43%	57%

Table 14
Attendance at churches and denominations in England and Wales 1979 to 2005

Opinion poll evidence also suggests women are more religious. A poll conducted in 1990 (Brierley, 2005) found that 84% of women believed in God, compared to 64% of men.

Evidence on New Age beliefs produced by Paul Heelas (2005) suggests that its followers are overwhelmingly female (as well as middle-aged or older).

Modood (1997) found in the Fourth National Survey of Ethnic Minorities that Muslim women were more likely to say religion was important to them than men, but men were more likely to attend mosques. However, this could partly be because some mosques do not welcome women.

Religious participation and attitude to risk

Alan Miller and John Hoffman (1995) identify two main theories explaining women's greater religiosity.

1. **Differential socialisation**. According to this view, women are taught to be more submissive and passive than men and these characteristics are associated with being more religious. Traditional religions tend to expect their followers to be passive and obedient. Research in the USA suggests that the less passive and obedient men are, the less likely they are to be involved in religion than other men.
2. **Structural location**. This is the view that women take more part in religion because of their social **roles**. Men are more likely to be the full-time **breadwinner** while women are more likely to be housewives, work part-time and bring up children. This gives women more time for church-related activities. Furthermore, women who do not have paid jobs and may have a need for a role that provides a sense of personal identity, and religion can fulfil this role. Taking children to church is also an extension of the mother role, since women tend to be the primary carers.

They go on to quote research, which suggests that even when these two factors are taken into account it does not fully explain why women are more religious than men. They argue that a third factor is important as well: attitude to **risk**.

Research suggests that men are more willing to take risks than women.

Not being religious can be seen as risk-taking behaviour because of the possibility that it may lead to failure to enter heaven. Miller and Hoffman's research shows that both men and women who are risk averse have high levels of religiosity.

Steve Bruce: Gender, religion and secularisation

Bruce (1996) argues that religion has an affinity with many aspects of femininity, such as those that make women less goal-orientated, more cooperative and less domineering. These attributes fit not just with traditional religion but also with the spiritual beliefs of the New Age. Women are particularly attracted to the healing and channelling aspects of the New Age, whereas men tend to be more interested in parapsychology.

Bruce believes the modern world has a sharp divide between the **public sphere** (paid work and politics) and the **private sphere** (the domestic world of the family and personal life). He supports the theory of secularisation, which argues not just that religion is declining, but also that it is retreating from the public sphere towards the private sphere. Because women are more closely connected with the private sphere than men, women are more likely to remain involved in traditional religions. Women tend to become involved in traditional churches because they have a particular interest in the socialisation of the next generation and the control of sexuality.

Bruce believes there are differences in which type of religion continues to appeal to women according to their social class.

1. **Working-class** women tend to continue to support religions, which believe in an all-powerful God and in which they are quite passive.
2. **Middle-class** women have more experience of controlling their lives and are more attracted to the New Age in which individuals can develop their own spirituality.

Essential notes

The theory of secularisation is defined in different ways. Some sociologists argue that religion is not really declining, it is just becoming more privatised.

Examiners' notes

These are really useful points linking class and gender to religious participation.

Key study
Linda Woodhead (2005): Gendering secularisation

Like Bruce, Woodhead believes that secularisation reduced the involvement of men in traditional religion as they became increasingly involved in the **rationalised** modern world.

As men withdrew from churches, they became increasingly feminised, and began to place more emphasis on love, care and relationships. Then from the 1970s onwards, increasing numbers of married women returned to paid work where they too were exposed to the rationalised culture of employment. As a result, the number of women attending church also began to decline rapidly.

This helps to explain the rapid reduction in church attendance in recent decades.

Woodhead believes that women still remain more religious than men, partly because the emphasis on relationships within churches remains, but also because New Age beliefs helped to resolve the identity problems of women combining paid work with caring roles.

Ethnicity and religious participation

Statistics on ethnicity and religion

The UK census provides statistical data on **ethnicity** and religious **identity**.

	Christian	Buddhist	Hindu	Jewish	Muslim	Sikh	No religion
White	75.89	0.12	0.02	0.83	0.38	0.01	15.34
Black or Black British	71.1	0.13	0.26	0.08	9.33	0.05	7.66
Indian	4.89	0.18	45.0	0.06	12.7	29.06	1.7
Pakistani	1.09	0.03	0.08	0.05	92.01	0.05	6.16
Bangladeshi	0.50	0.06	0.60	0.05	92.48	0.0	0.43
Chinese	21.56	15.12	0.07	0.05	0.33	0.03	52.60
All	71.75	0.28	1.06	0.50	2.97	0.63	14.81

Table 15

Religious identity by % of population in the 2001 census (England and Wales)

Not surprisingly, religious identity tends to reflect the dominant religions in the country of origin for minority ethnic groups (for example, Hinduism in the case of Indian ethnic minorities and Islam for Pakistani and Bangladeshi minorities).

- Survey research from 1997 (Modood et al.) looked at participation as well as identification. It found that African-Caribbeans had high rates of participation in 20th century sects such as Seventh Day Adventists and the New Testament Church of God.
- The survey also found that there were big differences in the importance attached to religion, e.g. only 11% of white members of the Church of England saw religion as very important in their lives, compared to 71% of Caribbean members of New Protestant churches, 43% of Hindus and 74% of Muslims.
- Minority ethnic groups, with the exception of the Chinese, were all more likely to attend places of worship than whites.

Key study

John Bird: Explanations for high levels of religiosity

John Bird identifies five important reasons why minority ethnic groups are more likely to be religious than the majority white population in Britain.

1. Many members of minority ethnic groups originate in societies that have high levels of religiosity, such as Pakistan and the Caribbean.
2. Belonging to a minority ethnic group within a society means that religion can be an important basis for a sense of community and solidarity. It can give members a point of contact, sense of identity and introduce them to potential marriage partners.
3. Minority groups may see religion as a way of maintaining cultural identity in terms of traditions such as food, language, art, music and so on.

4. **Socialisation** can lead to strong pressure on children to maintain religious commitment.
5. Religious beliefs may also be a way of coping with a sense of oppression. For example, Bird quotes a study by Ken Pryce, which examined how Pentecostalism acted as a way of helping some members of the African-Caribbean community in Bristol to cope with low pay and racial discrimination.

Ethnic minority religion, secularisation, and revival

Steve Bruce (1995) accepts that ethnic minorities are more religious than whites in modern Britain, but believes that their religiosity is more an expression of community solidarity than of deep religious commitment. He argues that ethnic minority religious observance stems from both:

- **cultural defence** – using religion as a way of protecting identity in an essentially hostile environment
- **cultural transition** – religion is used to cope with the upheaval of migration.

Bruce believes that, over time, the generally secular nature of British society will erode the importance of religion for ethnic minorities.

George Chryssides (1994) takes a more complex view. He identifies three possible paths for immigrants and their descendants in terms of religion:

1. **Apostasy** – beliefs are abandoned in a hostile environment.
2. **Accommodation** – religious beliefs are adapted to take account of the changed situation.
3. **Renewed vigour** – religion is reasserted more strongly than ever as a response to actual or perceived hostility.

Chryssides believes that the general pattern in the UK has been accommodation and renewed vigour; for example, accommodations such as Muslim women dressing modestly but still fashionably, or increased vigour, for example, finding new converts.

Gilles Kepel (1994) argues that there has been a general religious revival in the world for both minority and majority religions. He argues that Muslims have retained and strengthened their faith in response to an upsurge of Islamic beliefs throughout the world.

Policy Studies Institute Survey

Some evidence to evaluate these competing claims is provided by the Policy Studies Institute Survey (Modood et al., 1997).

The survey found that younger Chinese, white and African-Caribbean people were considerably less likely than older members of these groups to see religion as very important. For other ethnic groups, younger people were marginally less likely than their elders to see religion as very important. Thus the survey found evidence that religion was in decline from generation to generation, but at different rates in different ethnic groups. Despite this, the survey also found that religion remained much stronger in some groups, particularly Muslims, than in the population as a whole.

Essential notes

More detailed discussion of issues relating to secularisation and some useful evaluation of Bruce is on page 47.

Examiners' notes

Introduce fundamentalism to develop the analysis and evaluation for essay questions on this topic.

Essential notes

This evidence is not clear-cut; it suggests some overall weakening in the importance of religion, but not much.

Secularisation part 1

Defining secularisation

Many classic sociologists have argued that the growth of **scientific** knowledge along with **industrialisation** would lead to **secularisation**.

Secularisation has been defined in a wide variety of ways. Bryan Wilson (1966) defined it as 'the process whereby religious thinking, practice and institutions lose social significance'.

However, Steve Bruce (2002) says 'there is no one secularisation theory. Rather there are clusters of descriptions and explanations that cohere reasonably well'.

José Casanova (2003) distinguishes between two general approaches to defining secularisation:

1. An emphasis on the declining importance of religion in terms of the **social structure** and the significance of religion in society generally. This often involves the separation of religious life from the **public sphere** so that it becomes a private matter.
2. Using the term secularisation more narrowly to refer to the decline of religious belief and practices amongst individuals.

Glock and Stark (1969) argue that there are multiple aspects of secularisation, partly because there is no general agreement about what characterises a truly religious society. Different aspects of secularisation will be dealt with individually.

Classical theorists and secularisation

Sociologists from a wide variety of perspectives have argued that secularisation either was already taking place, or would take place in the future. Their views are summarised in table 16.

Theorists	Causes of secularisation	Form secularisation would take
Karl Marx	The eventual production of a **communist** society in which there were no **classes**.	The complete disappearance of religion, which would no longer be needed.
Émile Durkheim	Industrialisation leading to a greater **division of labour** and the decline of **mechanical solidarity** (based on similarity) and an increase in **organic solidarity** (based upon mutual interdependence).	The gradual reduction in the importance of religion for providing shared beliefs and therefore the integration of society. Education would partly take its place. Religion would survive but become less **functionally** important.

Theorists	Causes of secularisation	Form secularisation would take
Max Weber	The **rationalisation** of the modern world, in which people become primarily concerned with planning the most efficient ways of achieving their objectives. This would be caused by the development of science, the increasing importance of **bureaucratic** organisations, and the rational, planned nature of **capitalist society**.	The gradual reduction in the importance of faith and the increased emphasis upon knowledge based on evidence and actions designed to achieve goals.

Table 16
Classical views of secularisation

Comte also believed that scientific (**positivist**) beliefs would gradually replace faith (see pp 10–11).

Religious participation: church attendance and membership in the UK

Researchers who emphasise the decline of religious belief and practice have used data relating to religious participation as evidence to support their case.

- The 1851 Census of Churches found that just under 40% of the population attended church on a typical Sunday. In 2005, Brierley found that just 6.8% of the adult population regularly attended church.
- Between 1979 and 2005, attendance at Catholic, Anglican, United Reformed and Orthodox churches declined by nearly 50%.
- Between 1979 and 2005, attendance at free churches such as Methodist, Pentecostalist and new churches declined by around 25%.
- Attendance at special Christian ceremonies has declined rapidly. In the 1930s over 90% of children were baptised; by 2000 this had dropped to 45%.

The decline in church membership has been as rapid as the decline in attendance for most Christian religions. However, the proportion of the population belonging to non-Christian religions doubled between 1975 and 2000 (Brierley, 2001).

Interpreting the evidence

Most of the above evidence seems to suggest secularisation is taking place, at least in the UK; however, there are question marks over the **validity** and **reliability** of the statistics.

- 19th-century statistics pose problems because the standards of data collection may not meet contemporary standards of reliability.
- Different criteria are used to record membership in different religions.
- UK statistics on church attendance are based upon an annual survey conducted on one day in November, which may not be typical of attendance at other times of year.

Examiners' notes

Make sure that you relate your answer to the particular wording of the question before bringing in any wider, relevant issues on secularisation.

Examiners' notes

It is very important to distinguish between reliability and validity and to be critical of statistics if you include them in an answer.

☞ This topic continues on the next two pages

The validity of using attendance statistics as a way of measuring religiosity is also open to question. In the 19th century people may have attended church as a sign of respectability without being truly religious. Today, people may attend church in order to get their children into a church school, even if they have no religious beliefs.

Furthermore, today, religion may be expressed in other ways. It may have become more **privatised**, with people practising religion or developing their own beliefs away from institutions.

Religious participation outside the UK

If the theory of secularisation is applied globally, then the evidence does not support it (as it appears to in the UK). In the USA, religious participation is much higher than in most of Europe with some 40% attending church regularly. According to Brierley (2001) 34.5% of the world population were Christian in 1990 and by 2000 this had declined only slightly to 33%. The proportion has declined in Europe but increased in Africa, Latin America and Asia. Brierley also says there has been a big increase in the proportion of the world who are Islamic. His figures suggest a small decline in the proportion of people who are atheists and, therefore, a small increase in the total number of religious people in the world.

Religious belief

Membership and attendance provide only one way of measuring religious belief, since people may be religious outside the context of organised religion.

Opinion poll evidence does suggest that religious belief has declined. The table below shows that between 1947 and 2000 belief in God declined substantially, although general spiritual beliefs may have partly replaced more traditional beliefs in God.

Examiners' notes

If the question doesn't specify a particular place (e.g. the UK) make sure you broaden your answer to include international and global trends.

Essential notes

This opinion poll evidence suggests something of a shift away from traditional religion towards more generalised spiritual beliefs. This fits in with the ideas of Heelas and Woodhead.

Table 17
Belief in God in the UK, 1947 to 2000

	1947	2000
There is a personal God	45%	26%
There is some sort of spirit or life force	39%	21%
There is something there	Not applicable	23%
I don't really know what to think	16%	12%
I don't really think there is any sort of god, spirit or life force	Not applicable	15%

Essential notes

Supporters of the secularisation theory found the figures for those claiming a Christian affiliation unconvincing, arguing that people may be saying more about their background than actual religious beliefs.

Steve Bruce (2001) argues that those who say 'there is something there' are not really expressing strong or significant beliefs, therefore the opinion poll data shows significant weakening of religious beliefs.

However, the 2001 census in Britain found that most of the population did profess to belong to a religion. Of those answering (and 92% chose to answer the question), 71.6% said they were Christian, 2.7% Muslim, 1% Hindu, 0.6% Sikh, 0.5% Jewish, 0.3% Buddhist, and 0.3% other religions. Only 15.5% said they had no religion.

However, the validity of this data may be questioned, since over 390 000 people stated that they were Jedis or Jedi Knights.

Also, many of those stating their religion may have a very weak affiliation. In contrast, survey research in 2003 found that 41% said they had no religion.

Religious pluralism

Some researchers imply that the truly religious society has one faith and one church. This situation may be characteristic of small-scale societies such as the Australian Aborigines studied by Durkheim, but in modern industrial societies **religious pluralism**, the existence of many different faiths, is more typical.

Supporters of the secularisation theory, such as Steve Bruce, suggest that this creates a situation where religion is no longer a central feature of society but more a matter of personal choice. Bruce (2002) claims that, as a consequence, **strong religion**, which dominates people's lives, declines and is largely replaced by **weak religion**, which involves tolerance of different beliefs and has limited influence over people's lives.

To Bruce, **fragmented** and pluralistic societies such as the modern UK do not lend themselves to having a religion that exercises a strong influence.

However, critics of the secularisation theory believe that religious pluralism is not incompatible with a strongly religious society. People may have different beliefs but hold them very strongly. For example, in Northern Ireland, Christianity is more strongly followed than in England even though there is a major division between Catholics and Protestants.

Ethnicity and religious diversity

On the face of it, minority **ethnic groups** in Britain seem to contradict the theory of secularisation because they appear to have stronger religious beliefs than white British people (see page 48). However, Steve Bruce (1996) believes that greater participation is not the result of deep religious conviction, but serves a particular function for minority ethnic and migrant groups. These functions are:

1. **Cultural defence**. Where two communities are in conflict and have different beliefs, religion becomes a way of asserting ethnic pride. Similarly, when a minority ethnic group feels some hostility from the wider society, religion can be a way of achieving community solidarity.
2. **Cultural transition**. Religion can also be useful where people have to adjust their identity to deal with their changed situation. For example, Asian and African-Caribbean migrants to Britain can use mosques, temples and churches as centres for their communities.

To Bruce, these processes keep religion relevant but do not create a genuinely religious society. However, Brown (1992) disagrees and argues that ethnic defence is a crucial function of religion in the modern world, and because it leads to a revival of religion it creates more religious societies.

Similarly, Chryssides (1994) finds little evidence of decline in religion amongst ethnic minorities. Very few have abandoned their religion and become **apostates**; instead most have continued their religious beliefs, with some **accommodation** to their changed situation.

Examiners' notes

Include a discussion of different types of organisation (including sects, cults and new religious movements) if you are asked about secularisation and religious pluralism.

Examiners' notes

You can flesh out answers on this topic using page 48, which discusses ethnicity and participation.

Secularisation part 2

Sects, cults and secularisation

Supporters of the theory of secularisation do not see the existence and apparent growth of **sects**, **new religious movements** and **cults** as providing any significant evidence against the decline in the importance of religion.

- Bryan Wilson (1982) argues that such religious movements and organisations are 'almost irrelevant' to society as a whole. Their members live in their own enclosed encapsulated little worlds, which are of little influence or interest to those who are not members. He suggests they largely provide religion for 'dropouts', membership numbers are small and membership is often short-lived.
- Peter Berger (1970) described sects as 'islands in a secular sea'. He argued that strong religions can only survive and maintain their beliefs if they separate themselves from the largely secular wider society through living in communes.
- Steve Bruce (2002) argues that the small numbers joining such movements are a fraction of the numbers leaving mainstream **churches**. The most popular world-accommodating groups such as TM, Erhard Seminars Training (EST) and Hare Krishna have only a few thousand members in the UK and they have much less impact on people's lives than traditional religions do.

However, others see the vitality of these types of religion as evidence against secularisation.

- Andrew Greeley (1972) sees the growth of new religious movements as part of the process of **resacrilisation** – the emergence of a renewed interest in, and belief in, the sacred – taking place in societies such as Britain and the USA.
- Statistics do suggest some increase in the number of members of sects, cults, new religious movements and churches, which do not believe in the Holy Trinity (nontrinitarian churches). The following estimates were compiled by Brierley (2005).

Examiners' notes

In an essay question on sects and secularisation, you could discuss the contrasting viewpoints of Wilson, Berger and Bruce as opposed to Greeley, and include some statistical evidence.

Group	2000	2005
Church of Scientology	144 400	165 000
ISKCON (Krishna Consciousness)	9 000	10 500
Satanism	750	800
Baha'i	5 900	6 200
Buddhism	49 600	54 000
Zoroastrianism	3 200	3 250
All new religious movements	29 503	37 412
Nontrinitarian churches	539 968	547 178

Table 18
Religious membership of selected new religious movements and non-Christian religions, 2000 and 2005

According to Brierley's figures, the active membership of nontrinitarian and other religions (including ethnic minority religions) rose from 2.4% of the population in 2000 to 3.1% in 2010.

Secularisation and the New Age

Steve Bruce (1996) does not see the growth of the **New Age** as posing a threat to the validity of the theory of secularisation. He believes that New Age beliefs are weak, largely personal and have little or no influence on the wider society. However, others argue that a significant revival of religious and spiritual belief is taking place through the New Age.

Key study
Paul Heelas and Linda Woodhead: The Kendal Project

Paul Heelas and Linda Woodhead (2005) conducted a detailed study of religious beliefs in Kendal, a Cumbrian town close to the Lake District. They collected data on every religious group in the town, as well as all New Age activities they could find. They found that more people were taking part in spiritually-inclined New Age activities than were attending Anglican churches.

They argue that a **spiritual revolution** is underway in which the **congregational domain** (worship by congregations in conventional churches) is declining and the **holistic milieu** (informal networks through which people take part in New Age activities) is growing. Based on current trends, they estimate that the New Age may become more popular than all conventional churches put together by around 2020.

They argue that, overall, **subjectivisation** is taking place in religion, spiritual beliefs and society generally. This involves people emphasising their own choices rather than following instructions from authorities. The New Age is appealing because it allows individuals to choose the spiritual beliefs that fit with their own personal views and lifestyle. As a result, people are moving away from traditional religions where there is little choice about what to believe or how to worship. Rather than secularisation taking place, they suggest there has simply been a shift in the type of religious beliefs that people follow.

Secularisation, disengagement and differentiation

Some sociologists see secularisation more broadly than in terms of individual beliefs and participation in religious organisations. They focus on the declining significance of religion in society.

The **disengagement** of religion involves the withdrawal of the church from wider society. As the church loses **power**, wealth, prestige and influence, it becomes less involved in politics and social policy.

Steve Bruce (2002) links these changes to the process of **social differentiation** in which separate spheres of social life develop. In Western societies, the logic of capitalist production with an emphasis on profit and efficiency dominates. Religious and spiritual views are **marginalised** and become part of a separate and less important aspect of society. Churches are no longer the focal point for diverse communities as a whole, but rather centres for particular minority groups.

Examiners' notes

Check the wording of a question to see whether it is legitimate to include the New Age in an answer. Remember that it is debatable whether the New Age can be seen as religious; comment on this in discussions.

Essential notes

This is a crucial study, but a controversial one. It is debatable how far Kendal is typical of other parts of the country – it may attract the kind of people more likely to be interested in the New Age. Nevertheless, it is an immensely useful piece of research, which offers insights into the whole possible direction of change of religious belief in the UK and similar societies.

Examiners' notes

Interpret the question carefully to see if it is about individual participation and belief or if you should focus on the role of religious institutions.

This topic continues on the next two pages

Examiners' notes

You can develop your discussion of fundamentalism using material from pages 28–29.

Examiners' notes

Use plenty of technical terms rather than everyday language. The glossary provides meanings for terms like disengagement, social differentiation, structural differentiation and generalised.

Examiners' notes

A question may ask you to combine a discussion of science with a discussion of religion. These notes are a starting point, but you will also need to look in detail at the theory of postmodernism.

Essential notes

Weber's study, *The Protestant Ethic and the Spirit of Capitalism*, suggested that certain types of religion, particularly Calvinist Protestantism, helped to produce the capitalist system. This in turn led to disenchantment, the development of scientific rationalism and the decline of religion.

However, critics of the secularisation theory argue that such views are misleading.

Casanova (1994) believes that religion is still important in public life. In the 1980s, religion was linked to conflicts such as those between Jews and Muslim Palestinians in the Middle East and between Protestants and Catholics in Northern Ireland. More recently, **fundamentalism** demonstrates the continued political importance of religion both in the USA and in the Muslim world.

Talcott Parsons (1965) accepted that the church had lost many of its former **functions** in a process he called **structural differentiation**. For example, it has less responsibility for education and welfare than it did in the past. However, he believed that in the USA the church remained very important because Christian values had been **generalised** – they have been absorbed into the culture of the society and underpin the American way of life, the **value consensus**, the legal system and so on.

Secularisation, science and rationality

A number of sociologists have argued that society has been undergoing a process of desacrilisation, in which supernatural forces are no longer seen as controlling the world, and action is no longer directed by religious beliefs. This particularly involves an increasing reliance upon scientific knowledge.

This view was supported by Comte (1986) who believed that societies started off with theological belief systems, based upon religion, but ended up with positivist belief systems, based on objective science (see page 10).

Key study
Max Weber: Disenchantment and rational action

The most influential supporter of the belief that religious belief systems will be replaced by non-religious beliefs was Max Weber (1963). Weber believed that capitalism was characterised by planning in order to maximise profits, and by organisation using bureaucracies. (Bureaucracies are organisations that aim to achieve specific ends using a **hierarchy** of officials and rules.)

In the modern world, therefore, **rational action**, based upon deliberate and precise calculation and logic, becomes dominant. At the same time, science develops and explains natural phenomena, which were once mysterious. This leads to **disenchantment**; the modern world is no longer charged with mystery and magic.

In this situation there is little room for superstition or religious faith; scientific rationality becomes dominant, and religion gradually declines.

Steve Bruce (2002) also sees **rationalisation** as very important in causing secularisation.

He argues that technological advances have given individuals a greater sense of control over the natural world and less need to resort to supernatural explanations. Prayer becomes a last resort when scientific and rational solutions to problems have failed.

However, some sociologists question the view that science and rationalism have replaced superstition and faith.

- The Kendal Project (Heelas and Woodhead, 2005) suggests that non-rational New Age beliefs are becoming increasingly influential.
- **Postmodernism** argues that we have become sceptical of scientific rationality. People are increasingly aware of the failures of science and the negative side effects of science and technology. They therefore reject all **metanarratives** (including science and traditional religions) and instead pick and choose their own beliefs, many of which contain a spiritual element. People become '**spiritual shoppers**' with an interest in the non-rational.

Conclusion on secularisation

There are a number of possible conclusions that can be made about the theory of secularisation.

1. How convincing the theory is depends upon which parts of the world you are discussing. In Western Europe, religious participation, belief and the influence of churches all seem to have declined. However, in most other parts of the world, including the USA, the Muslim world, Latin America and Africa, religion may actually be getting stronger.

2. The conclusion may depend upon how you define secularisation. For example, religion may decline in one way (the influence of religion on society might decrease), but not in another (more people might start to believe in religion). Also, traditional religious participation and beliefs may decline, but new types of spirituality might increase.
   Therefore, whether secularisation is seen as taking place depends on whether you are using a broad, **inclusive** definition of religion, which sees New Age spirituality as a religion, or an exclusive definition that does not see this as a religion.

3. The evidence could be seen as inadequate to decide definitively whether secularisation is taking place or not. For example, there is a lack of historical evidence about how strong the beliefs of individuals were in the past. They may have attended church because they were compelled to or as a mark of respectability. Keith Thomas (1977) argues that **pre-industrial** England contained a lot of scepticism about religion, and the extent to which religion has declined since can therefore be exaggerated.

4. Glock and Stark (1969) argue that it is too simplistic to either support or criticise secularisation; instead the concept has to be broken down and related to specific places before it is possible to reach a conclusion. There is not therefore one conclusion, but many.

Examiners' notes

You must relate your conclusion to the question, it must be based upon what you have said in your answer, and it should show that you have considered conflicting viewpoints.

Modernity, postmodernity and religion

The theory of postmodernity

The theory of postmodernity argues that society has passed, or begun to pass, from the modern to the **postmodern** era.

The modern era is characterised by the importance of science and rationality, the belief that progress is both possible and desirable, and the belief that humans can plan, using theories to make the world a better place.

According to Lyotard (1979), the leading theorist of postmodernity, the postmodern era is characterised by a decline in metanarratives. (A metanarrative is a 'big story' about how the world works, how it can be improved and how people should behave, for example, communism, Christianity or science.) However, because of the disastrous effects these metanarratives have had, such as the devastation produced by religious wars, communism in the Soviet Union, fascism in Germany and the damage to the environment caused by technological advance, people are no longer happy to accept them.

> **Key study**
> **Zygmunt Bauman: Religion and postmodernity**
>
> Bauman (1992) argues that in modernity people sought universal truths. In postmodernity, people do not accept the idea of universal truths or that other people should have authority over them. Instead they believe they should have choice over what to believe and how to behave.
>
> Without a generally accepted set of moral rules or principles, people have to make their own ethical choices. Morality therefore becomes privatised: a matter of individual preference.
>
> Nevertheless, people still want expert guidance on what rules to adopt since it is too difficult to make up their own beliefs entirely from scratch. They look to religious leaders as experts in morality to help them form their own beliefs. However, they do not have to accept the teachings of the leaders followed by their parents; they can choose which religious or spiritual leaders to take notice of for themselves.
>
> This leads to religious pluralism, in which a wide variety of religious and spiritual beliefs exist; people can change their beliefs quite rapidly and mix different types of beliefs together.

Criticisms of Bauman

Beckford (1996) claims that Bauman exaggerates the changes in the importance of religion. He suggests that religion has remained continuously important through history, rather than declining greatly in modernity and reviving dramatically in postmodernity.

Beckford also argues that Bauman contradicts himself by arguing that people wish both to follow leaders and to create their own morality.

Key study

David Lyon: *Jesus in Disneyland*

David Lyon (2000) believes that the growth of postmodernity involves the development of **globalisation**, information technology and a consumer society. These trends give people greater choice, including a choice of gods.

Because of these changes, religion is becoming another aspect of **consumption**. People are not willing to be forced to accept the authority of Christianity or any other religion, but they are willing to choose a religious narrative (or story) that appeals to them. For example, in Canada 75% of people do not attend church regularly but 80% of non-attenders still have religious beliefs.

Lyon gives as an example of the movement of religion to the sphere of consumption, the holding of religious events, such as the harvest day crusade, at Disneyland in California. This mixes religion with the consumer fantasy world of Disney.

Lyon believes that **dedifferentiation** is taking place – a blurring of the boundaries and differences between different parts of social life. In this case, the distinction between religion and popular culture is diminishing. Religion is no longer a social institution in which people have to take part, but rather a cultural resource on which people can draw if they wish.

Postmodernity and the New Age

There are a number of features of the New Age that could be seen as typical of postmodernity. These include a move away from traditional religious metanarratives, and a blurring of the boundary between religion and popular culture.

However, Paul Heelas believes that the New Age is part of modernity rather than postmodernity, arguing it is an extreme form of **individualism**, a crucial aspect of modernity, and it does involve a metanarrative.

Conclusion

Although there is disagreement about whether we have entered a postmodern era, there is widespread agreement that significant changes have taken place in society and religion. Whether or not religion is declining, there is little doubt that it is becoming a more personal and individual matter in Western societies.

Essential notes

It is a matter of interpretation as to whether the New Age reflects a move to a postmodern society.

General tips for the Beliefs in Society exam

The Beliefs in Society examination paper (SCLY3) consists of two compulsory questions and one further question to choose from two options. You will have 1½ hours to complete the paper. The maximum mark for this paper is 60, so, once you have taken off time for reading, this is less than 1½ minutes per mark. The exam carries 40% of the A2 marks.

You will be given one Item to read, to help you with question 02. Before you start this question, you should read the Item carefully to identify points or issues that you can use. Remember, the Item is there only to provide you with a starting point; this is **not** a comprehension. It will, however, give you some starting points for question 02, such as key words and phrases you may be able to use.

For each question there are more marks awarded for AO2 skills of interpretation, application, analysis and evaluation than there are for AO1 knowledge and understanding skills. At A2 level, you are expected to show that you can interpret questions well and then apply appropriate material in your answer. You are also expected to show good analysis and evaluation; you need to unpack and discuss issues, not just describe theories and research. You can also show these skills by having a clear focus on the question, rather than writing in general about the topic area.

- **Question 01** is a short question worth 9 marks. You will be asked to 'identify and explain' three things. These may be problems, characteristics, ways, reasons, etc. You will gain 1 mark for each of three correct identifications, then 2 marks for each of three satisfactory explanations. Each explanation will probably need one or two sentences.
- **Question 02** is worth 18 marks, so slightly less is required here than for the long essay in question 03. It is also connected to the Item. You will be asked to use the Item and therefore you will not be able to gain top marks if you do not do so. You should try to build on the Item by developing some of the ideas put forward. However, the words 'and elsewhere' mean that you are expected to contribute a lot of your own ideas – the Item will not provide everything you need. To 'assess' you must show evaluation and judgement. 12 of the marks for this essay are for AO2 skills and only 6 marks are for AO1 skills. Make sure you include some references to the wording of the question, to sociological concepts and perspectives, and that you cover all the elements in the question. Start with a short introduction of the most important elements of the question and end with a brief conclusion, bringing all the main themes of your essay together.
- **Questions 03** and **04** are essay questions and you must choose to answer one of these. They will be 'free-standing' – they will not have an Item to refer to. These questions are worth 33 marks: 15 for AO1 skills; 9 for interpretation and application; 9 for analysis and evaluation. As with question 02, you will be asked to 'assess'. Make sure that you focus clearly on the question set. As this is a long essay, make sure you plan what you are going to say before you start.

When writing your answer to question 03 or 04 (and also for question 02), you should look back regularly to the question. Make sure you have followed all of the instructions and covered all of the issues included in the question. Some essays have two or more parts. You will not gain top marks if you do not deal with each part. It's also very important to focus on the question set. Do not be tempted to write an essay about all you know on the topic in question, or to spend time writing at a tangent to the question – try to use your material to focus on the issues.

Beliefs in Society (sample exam paper 1)

Read Item A below and answer parts (01) to (03) that follow.

Item A

For some people, religion plays an important role in their lives; for others, its role is minimal. One factor that seems to be important here is that of age, shown clearly by statistics on religious belief and participation.

In 2005 the English Church Census showed that the number of people attending church regularly had fallen from 5.4 million in 1979 to 3.2 million in 2005. Over the same period, the average age of churchgoers had increased from 37 to 45. The age group that had declined the least was those over 65 years. In fact, 12% of churchgoers were 75 or over. In contrast, the age groups that had declined the most in this period were the 15–19 and 20–29 cohorts. For these age groups, the numbers had fallen by over 60%.

Although these figures apply only to the Christian churches, other religious groups in the United Kingdom also show significant differences between young and old in terms of religious belief, though these differences are less marked among the Pakistani and Bangladeshi communities.

Questions

01 Identify and explain **three** ways in which religion can be seen to be patriarchal. **[9 marks]**

02 Using material from **Item A** and elsewhere, assess the reasons why the young seem less likely to believe and participate in religion than older people. **[18 marks]**

03 '*No matter how much it changes and varies from place to place, people always need religion.*'
To what extent do sociological arguments and evidence support this view? **[33 marks]**

01 *Identify and explain three ways in which religion can be seen to be patriarchal.* **[9 marks]**

A good answer. Three appropriate ways are identified and satisfactorily explained. Other appropriate ways might include: religious ideologies; women worshippers kept apart; taboos about women, seen as polluting; genital mutilation.

Mark: 3/3 + 3/3 + 3/3 = 9/9

- Positions in the hierarchies of established religions tend to be male-dominated. For example, the Catholic Church does not allow women to become priests. The Church of England now allows women to be vicars but many people are leaving the Church in protest at the possibility of women bishops.

- In some religions, there are stricter rules about how women must dress and behave, compared to men. For example, orthodox Jewish women have to keep to strict rules about their dress and hair. In some Islamic countries, women must wear the hijab or burka.

- Feminists argue that holy books are written by men and feature men. For example, in the Bible all the most significant Old Testament prophets are male while in the New Testament, all the apostles are men. When women are mentioned, they represent traditional and subordinate feminine roles, e.g. the Virgin Mary or Eve.

02 *Using material from* Item A *and elsewhere, assess the reasons why the young seem less likely to believe and participate in religion than older people.* **[18 marks]**

A good introduction, applying material from the Item to confirm patterns of participation.

The evidence suggests that the young are significantly less likely than the elderly to make up the congregations of the established churches, e.g. 47% of people aged over 50 say they belong to a religion compared with only 10% of 16–24 year olds. Young people are much more likely to be secularised compared with the older generation. This can be seen in Item A – the census of church attendance clearly shows that congregations in traditional Christian churches are ageing and that young people's attendance has declined by over 60%.

Two appropriate reasons are outlined clearly and two sources identified correctly.

One of the reasons suggested by Voas and Crockett to explain why these differences exist is because the elderly become more concerned about death and spiritual things – people seem to need to turn to religion more as they get older, and may feel they need an 'insurance' policy. Davie suggests that this may also be due to loneliness. The other main reason Voas and Crockett put forward is that the young are more susceptible to secularisation. They have grown up in a secular society, whereas the old grew up when religion was still seen as very important.

Evidence from minority ethnic groups, linked to the Item, is used as evaluation, with a point of counter-evaluation added. A good paragraph.

However, not all young people fit into this pattern. Item A shows that young Asians are more likely to have religious beliefs compared with young white people. Modood found that 67% of young Pakistanis and Bangladeshis valued the importance of Islam in their lives. Some young male Muslims seem to be very attracted by the anti-Western stance of fundamentalist Islam that sees Western societies as morally corrupt. However, Choudhury found that it was young men who were not very knowledgeable about Islam who were most easily radicalised. ☞

Another reason why young white people seem to participate in religious activity far less than older generations is suggested by the postmodernist Hervieu-Leger, who argues that younger people may have 'cultural amnesia' – they have not been socialised into religious stories and morality like the previous generations. They are not as likely to be sent to Sunday school, and religious teaching in schools is far less than it was. Despite this apparent decline, some types of beliefs and spirituality seem to appeal to the young, but they are interested in a much wider range of ideas, not just traditional religions. There is evidence that many young people are interested in New Age movements and ideas, such as crystals, holistic medicines, yoga and meditation. There is even a growth in popularity of films about vampires, ghosts and zombies!

Lynch argues that the young have more spiritual choices. They are exposed to more religious beliefs and groups, including NRMs, world-rejecting sects, New Age religions and other cults. So therefore they are the most likely to go 'spiritual shopping'. Young people may also be under other non-religious influences, such as drugs and music etc., that can also become a way of spiritual fulfilment.

Finally, young people have many more demands on their time compared with the past. Nowadays, sport can be played or watched on a Sunday, shopping centres are open, education goes on much longer etc. The younger generation therefore has a greater range of choice in terms of how to spend their time; they are also likely to have more money to do so compared with the older generation, so there's less time and energy for religion.

However, there is evidence that many young African-Caribbeans and Africans attend Pentecostal and Baptist churches. According to Nelson, they are attracted to these churches because they are lively and spontaneous with less of the formal rituals of the established churches that seem to turn them off. There is also evidence that younger adults, especially middle-class university-educated ones, are more likely to get involved with world-rejecting NRMs or sects, because they may be having what postmodernists call a 'crisis of meaning' – they are more likely to be unhappy with materialism and they may feel the world is morally corrupt.

Another reason for the difference is presented, and an alternative interpretation suggested.

Some repetition of the previous point, but there are also some useful new ideas here.

Some more practical reasons for the differences are suggested.

Two further points of evaluation, based on research and theory. No conclusion offered.

Overall, this is a good answer to the question. Both belief and participation are considered, though the distinction between the two could be made more clearly. Focus on the question is good and a number of relevant concepts are used. Focus is on the young, though more contrast with older people could be made, as in the question. The Item is used well. There is some good analysis and several well-made points of evaluation. Ethnic differences are outlined but the answer could usefully include some reference to gender and/or social class differences too. Links to theoretical perspectives could be more explicit.

Mark: 5/6 + 10/12 = 15/18

03 *'No matter how much it changes and varies from place to place, people always need religion.'*
To what extent do sociological arguments and evidence support this view? **[33 marks]**

A clear introduction, expanding on the question, plus a good explanation of functionalist views, clearly connected to the issue of 'need'.

The nature and influence of religion varies a great deal between different communities and societies. Some societies are considered to be very religious; others appear to have been secularised to the extent that religion is no longer seen as important. In terms of sociological theory, functionalist writers see religion, like every other institution, as filling certain human needs. Durkheim argued that it provides integration and social solidarity, through common values and norms. Functionalists see religion as an important agent of secondary socialisation that teaches people values and norms that are special because they are sacred. These 'moral codes' underpin social behaviour and tell us what is immoral and criminal. For example, they prepare children for life by teaching them the difference between right and wrong. If we all learn and keep to these moral codes it holds people closely together in a moral community. So for the functionalists at least, people (and societies) 'always need religion'.

A good paragraph, extending the application of functionalist theory but still linking this to 'need'.

Another functionalist, Malinowski, also argued that religion provides people with reassurance at times of crisis and danger, because it gives people the feeling that there is some control over events. So therefore this theory focuses on the ways in which religion fulfils our needs – to keep order in society and help us cope with things we don't understand. This is both for the individual and society.

An alternative theoretical perspective is offered, also linked clearly to the question. Good analysis and evaluation skills are shown.

In contrast, Marxists argue that religion only serves the needs of the ruling class as it legitimates their power over the poor, persuades the poor to blame themselves for their suffering, and provides hope in terms of an afterlife. This helps maintain the status quo and keeps the working class in their place. It does not serve the needs of the poor, because it leaves them in a state of false consciousness. Both these major perspectives on religion therefore see it as having a major role in people's lives to fulfil needs, but for the Marxists there would be no need for religion if capitalism is overthrown.

Further analysis using Weber and rationality.

A somewhat different approach is that of Max Weber, who suggested that religion served the needs of capitalism by promoting the values that allowed capitalism to grow and thrive. However, Weber went further in that he argued that the development of modern society would mean an increase in rationality and science, and therefore a declining need for religion. Science has produced explanations for events that were previously explained by religion.

A good link from Weber to secularisation. This process is linked consistently to the need for religion.

In the UK and many other European countries, the need for religion does appear to have declined over the last century, as a result of the rise of science and technology. This means that there is less need for religion to answer questions about life. At the same time modern societies have become more mobile and diverse. This has undermined religion because the church is no longer the centre of the local community and people are less likely to turn there for help when they are in trouble. This is the process of secularisation, that religious institutions and practices have lost their social significance. ☞

The idea that people always need religion has been challenged by secularisation. Church attendance statistics show a decline in religion. In 1851 40% of the population attended church, this was less than 8% by 2009. The number of baptisms, communions, confirmations and weddings in church have all fallen. The number of clergy has fallen too and so has their status in society. All of these factors suggest that the majority of British people no longer need religion.

However some sociologists suggest that statistics should not be trusted because religious beliefs are seen today as a private matter by many people. Davie says that many people are 'believing not belonging', they have beliefs but don't go to a church, but still the majority of people say they believe in God. There are also lots of alternative ways people can spend their time today, in addition to religion, such as shopping, sport, chat rooms, pubs and clubs, therefore religion has less influence over people today. There are also more and more different religions to choose from.

In other parts of the world, however, religion still has much power and influence, so it would appear that it is still needed by the population. Davie sees Europe as an exception. Even in the most capitalist country, the USA, religious attendance is high and seen as important in politics. However, Bruce argues that religion in the USA has become secularised internally, in other words it has stayed popular because it has become less religious. Americans will often change their religion, it doesn't matter so much which one it is. Some sociologists have argued that the USA is more religious because it is very unequal and insecure. This might fit with Marxist ideas of the way religion works.

Outside Europe, Marxist ideas might also explain the high levels of religion in poorer countries, where people feel they are threatened by famine, disease and disaster and so need comfort from religion. In some places, religious fundamentalism has grown. These are people who want to stick very closely to basic ideas and follow the literal truth of the scriptures. As a result they are very intolerant of other religions. Sociologists like Bruce and Giddens see the increase in fundamentalism as a reaction to globalisation and change. They feel threatened by modernisation and things like permissiveness and equality. This may therefore be the result of new needs arising.

Religion can also fill the need for group identity. Cultural transition is the way people have to adapt when they go to a new country or city, and cultural defence is the way a group can maintain its ethnic identity in a new place or against a foreign power. Religious participation can be very important in these circumstances. Modood shows that the first generations of immigrants in the UK are very religious, but as we move down through the generations religion becomes less important.

However, Greely argues new religious movements in Britain are growing and this shows that religion is reviving, especially in evangelical churches. These churches offer religion that is less formal and more spontaneous than the old traditional churches. Postmodernists agree with this. They say that new age religions are also growing because people have become dissatisfied with ☞

Two further points about secularisation, but these are at a tangent to the question and add little to the answer. More could be made of the reference to widespread belief.

This is a good paragraph in which there is an attempt to address the 'place to place' aspect of the question. Another example, the USA, is used, evaluated, and connected to theory.

As in the previous paragraph, other societies are suggested in contrast. A possible link between growth of fundamentalism and the need for religion is suggested. This point could be developed.

Two useful concepts are introduced and their relevance briefly explained.

Further evaluation is provided and another perspective. A link is made to the issue of need, but there is little in the way of a conclusion.

materialism and are looking for something more spiritual in their lives. This has resulted in increased interest in different sects and cults and also lots of new age therapies. So perhaps the needs are still there but are being filled by a different sort of religion.

Overall, this is a good answer, which clearly addresses the question. A good range of arguments and evidence are produced. Although the main focus is on modern Britain, there is an attempt to deal with the differences in time and place referred to in the question, through discussion of religion in the USA and fundamentalist religion. This aspect could be dealt with more thoroughly.

There is good knowledge and understanding shown of the topic area, with a very good range of concepts, sources and application of theory. Good interpretation and application are shown with reference throughout on the need for religion. The writer has not been tempted to focus only on the process of secularisation. There is evidence of sound analysis and a number of valid points of evaluation.

Mark: 13/15 + 8/9 + 7/9 = 28/33

Total marks: 9 + 15 + 28 = 52/60 = Grade A

Beliefs in Society (sample exam paper 2)

Read Item A below and answer parts (01) to (03) that follow.

Item A

Until recently, the dominant arguments within the sociology of religion have been about the role religion plays in society and the extent to which religious practice and influence may or may not be declining in modern Western society.

However, postmodernists have now suggested that religion is changing, rather than declining. They argue that traditional religion based on the community has been replaced by a much more individual affair, based on personal choice. According to postmodernist writers, this change means that believers today are more likely to be private 'consumers' of religion, rather than members of a close religious community.

Questions

01 Identify and briefly explain **three** problems in measuring the extent of religious belief in society today. [**9 marks**]

02 Using material from **Item A** and elsewhere, assess the postmodernist view that the nature of religion in society today is becoming a matter of consumer choice. [**18 marks**]

03 Assess sociological explanations of the ways in which globalisation has affected the role of religion in different societies. [**33 marks**]

01 *Identify and briefly explain three problems in measuring the extent of religious belief in society today.* **[9 marks]**

Three problems have been successfully identified. The first identifier also provides a satisfactory explanation. However, the second identifier has no satisfactory explanation, and the third is only partially satisfactory. Other possible answers could include the lack of regular counts of believers and the fact that the concept of belief is not easy to define and operationalise.

Mark: 3/3 + 1/3 + 2/3 = 6/9

- There is no standardised measuring tool used by all religions to measure the extent of religious belief. Some measure religious belief by counting the number of times people attend religious ceremonies whilst others count members, i.e. people who are born into the church or who have been baptised etc. This means that measurements of religious belief are unreliable.

- Davie points out that many people believe in God but do not feel they need to belong to a church or religion. It's not seen as necessary.

- One of the main measurements of religious belief is attendance at church. However, Davie notes that people may get involved in religious institutions for other reasons.

02 *Using material from* Item A *and elsewhere, assess the postmodernist view that the nature of religion in society today is becoming a matter of consumer choice.* **[18 marks]**

A reasonable outline of some postmodernist ideas, though not linked to the notion of consumer choice.

Postmodernists believe that in recent years western societies have undergone major economic and cultural changes. We have changed from a modern to a postmodern society and this has had a big impact on the religious beliefs we hold. For example, in a traditional society, a person is born into a religion, they will learn about that religion from a young age and it will shape their personality. However, in modern society, people have become disillusioned with the stories, or metanarratives, of the major religions, and so traditional religion has experienced secularisation as people choose not to go to church. At the same time, postmodernists argue that New Age religions are now growing because people still want something spiritual in their lives. So religion may not be disappearing, but just changing to fit a postmodern society.

Some further development of postmodernist ideas.

Hervieu-Leger suggests that religion has declined due to 'cultural amnesia'. In the past, religion was handed down to children by the family, the school and Sunday school. But this tradition has now broken down. So children today are less likely to get a religious identity from their family, so they know much less about traditional religion.

This paragraph begins to address the question of religion and consumer choice.

Postmodernists argue that the emphasis in postmodern society is for the individual to make choices in their lives about their own personal identity. This has had a number of effects on the nature of religion. Firstly, Hervieu-Leger says that individual consuming has become more important than what religion you are born into. People no longer follow a religion without question or see religion as absolute truth. So therefore religion has become 'a matter of consumer choice'. Secondly, Hervieu-Leger says that people often decide to follow a religion today because they are joining a religion as part of their own personal spiritual journey. They are therefore making choices for themselves. She notes that some people, who she calls pilgrims, are likely to join ☞

'New Age' groups in a search for their own spirituality through meditation. Others, who she calls converts, join religious groups that give them a strong sense of belonging to a community, replacing the traditional type of religious community. This would include evangelical groups.

Another postmodernist writer is David Lyon, who argues that globalisation has had a massive effect on religion in postmodern society. He says that religious television has taken religion out of its local context. People can see and experience religion in their own sitting room. They no longer have to go to church – they can worship via television or on a computer. Lyon also says that globalisation has meant people can gain experience of more religions from different parts of the world, especially Eastern mystical religions that stress spiritual things rather than the worship of a God. Lyon believes that the UK is experiencing a 're-enchantment', i.e. a religious revival because of globalisation. So therefore he suggests that this is evidence against secularisation. Traditional religions have declined, but religion is still important to people. This has led to a growth in lots of different types of beliefs and spirituality. Globalisation means that these take a different form today compared with the past.

> Another postmodernist source is identified and explained well, but the opportunity is missed to show explicitly how this links to the question.

In particular, Lyon argues that religion has moved to the sphere of consumption; it is just another consumer item that we need to make a choice about. We become 'spiritual shoppers', choosing which bits of which faiths we want and add them to the other choices that make up our identity. People are looking for ways to show faith and spirituality outside the traditional churches.

> The vital link to the question is now made in this paragraph.

However, Steve Bruce (2002) argues that the impact of spiritual shopping and NRMs is exaggerated by postmodernists because these new movements are not as powerful as in the past. He also argues that religion in the media is not the same. People view programmes that confirm their existing beliefs – religious programmes don't make new converts. So therefore this new religion is 'weak' religion – it doesn't involve much commitment or passion, like going to church, and so doesn't affect people's lives very much. He argues that it provides evidence for secularisation rather than for re-enchantment.

> This paragraph offers some criticism of postmodernist ideas but is not specifically linked to consumer choice.

So overall postmodernist views of religion today do suggest that religion has become a consumer choice. People have become spiritual shoppers who consume beliefs from an array of religions and spiritual ideas available to them.

> A brief but good conclusion that links directly to the question.

This answer includes good accounts of several postmodernist views and focuses well on the question of consumerism at several points. However, this needs to be more consistent. Knowledge and understanding of the topic area is quite good and a good range of concepts and sources are used. There is some good analysis and a number of points of evaluation, though this could be related more closely to the issues raised by the question. (See page 71 – 'Note'.)

Other relevant issues might include: comparison with alternative views, fundamentalism, religious market theory, the relationship between religion and security, religion as cultural defence.

Mark 5/6 + 9/12 = 14/18

03 *Assess sociological explanations of the ways in which globalisation has affected the role of religion in different societies.* **[33 marks]**

A good introduction to the concept of globalisation. A weak link to religion.

Globalisation refers to the fact that the world is becoming more and more interconnected in many different ways, such as global communication, global markets and global media. Some believe that this is turning us into a global society, with fewer and fewer differences between us. Some sociologists believe that religion is one of the areas of society that are affected.

Further explanation of globalisation; no reference to religion.

In the past different communities and societies were separated from each other by time and space. Most people knew little of what was going on in other parts of the world. Today the world has shrunk because of the development of satellite communications and the internet and mass tourism has been spread by cheap air travel, so we can now keep in contact with people from many different cultures. Television programmes produced in the USA and other western countries are sent to many different countries.

Another aspect of globalisation. Still no reference to religion.

In addition, trade between countries has grown and there are a growing number of transnational companies that sell their goods all over the world, such as Coca-Cola, Nike or McDonald's. Goods are also produced all over the world, so what is the latest fashion in Britain may have been produced in India or China. And thousands of workers move about from one country to another in order to find work and a good standard of living.

Two aspects of globalisation are applied to religion.

So what effect does this have on religion? One of the possible effects is the loss of control over members of a religion. If people are moving away from their communities, their religious ties may weaken. They will also be more open to other religions or consumerism. The interaction of cultures may mean that traditional societies undergo a process of secularisation, just like many western countries, so religion declines. This interaction can work both ways. Research in Britain shows that many British people have been questioning traditional religion and becoming interested in eastern religions and New Age ideas.

A useful point about communication, but this is not applied to the question.

One of the most important changes as a result of globalisation is communication. The number of TV sets around the world has multiplied fast, and now the same is happening with the internet. Three-quarters of all the phones in Africa are mobiles and this has had many effects of modernisation of jobs, efficiency and keeping in touch when people move around more.

A valid point is made here about identity, but an opportunity is missed to show with examples the ways religion can act as cultural defence with examples.

Of course, not all the effects of globalisation are to make communities more and more similar. Sometimes more contact makes people feel that they are threatened and also their way of life is threatened, so conflict is produced. Religion is one of the ways that people can show resistance to being dominated by wealthier countries, by making religion a more important part of life and their community identity. In any case, just because someone in Africa wears Levi jeans and a Manchester United shirt doesn't mean they will automatically give up their religion or their identity. The idea of 'cultural defence' is used to describe one of the ways religion can be used against what is seen as a threat from outside.

Some people have turned to fundamentalism as a way of resisting – they see globalisation as threatening religious values and want to preserve ☞

the purity of their religion. Giddens says fundamentalists want to return to 'fundamental' faith, as close as possible to the holy scriptures, and obey them absolutely. Western values are seen as immoral and corrupt, so fundamentalism resists the globalisation of these. In some cases this has led to terrorism such as Al Qaeda's 9/11 attack on the twin towers.

Some of the changes have been less violent, however, but could still be linked to globalisation. For example, partly as a result of the massive spread of AIDS in Africa, the Pope has now had to say that condoms can be used to stop the spread of disease, something the Catholic church has always rejected in the past. Similarly, Muslims can now get Islamic mortgages from Islamic banks, something that was never allowed in the past.

> A couple of valid points are made about fundamentalism; these could usefully be developed. One appropriate source used.

> Another valid point is made about changes that may be due to interaction. No conclusion is offered.

Overall quite a good attempt to focus on the effects of globalisation on religion, though this focus is not apparent until paragraph 4. There is minimal reference to sociological theory or sources. The writer takes several different aspects of the process of globalisation and attempts to apply them to religion. Somewhat limited knowledge is therefore used to good effect. A number of concepts are used. There is evidence of some reasonable analysis and hints of evaluation.

The essay could be improved by more attention to sociological perspectives, such as Marxism, postmodernism and feminism. In addition, evidence could be provided through sources such as Nanda in India; Haynes' opposition to Giddens; Huntington on the 'clash of civilisations'.

Mark: 9/15 + 5/9 + 5/9 = 19/33

Total marks: 6 + 14 + 19 = 39/60 = Grade C

Note:
The answer to question 02 (18 marks) on the previous page is longer than the answer to question 03 (33 marks) on these pages. Make sure you allocate enough time to each question depending on the number of marks.

Improving your grade

The following examples show how you can improve your answers to the short questions for Beliefs in Society.

01 Identify and briefly explain **three** ways in which religion could be said to exert social control over members of society. **[9 marks]**

> Enough for a single identification mark but no explanation.

> Another identification point but does not explain how.

> Another identification point but does not explain how.
>
> **Mark: 1/3 + 1/3 + 1/3 = 3/9**

Weak answer

- Religion acts as social control because it is the opiate of the masses.

- Marxists say religion controls people in maintaining capitalism.

- Religion exerts social control through patriarchy because it enforces male domination.

> The idea of cushioning oppression is partially explained.

> Some explanation but not sufficient for full marks.

> Identification of point is satisfactory but very weak explanation.
>
> **Mark: 2/3 + 2/3 + 1/3 = 5/9**

Better answer

- Lenin called religion 'spiritual gin' because it acts to control people and help them forget.

- Marxist theory shows how religion is a conservative force that prevents social change because it promotes false consciousness.

- Religion reinforces the ways in which women are controlled through its teachings about men and women.

> Identification and explanation of the cushioning of oppression.

> Identification of point and explanation that shows how it operates.

> Identification of legitimation of patriarchy with appropriate examples and explanation.
>
> **Mark: 3/3 + 3/3 + 3/3 = 9/9**

Good answer

- Religion acts as the 'opiate of the people' because it stops people feeling so bad about their position. It 'cushions' oppression, because it helps people forget about their situation and makes them think they will have a better life in the afterlife.

- Marxist theory sees religion as an instrument of oppression because it tells the masses that both they and the ruling class have been put in their position by God, so they should not challenge this.

- Feminists argue that religion legitimates patriarchal power, for example in making strict rules about how women should dress that do not apply to men, such as covering heads or faces with a veil or a burka, and ruling that women aren't allowed to do many of the things men can.

Beliefs in Society

Accommodation	To Chryssides, compromising your religious beliefs in order to adapt to a new situation, e.g. migration
Alienation	A sense of being distanced from something so that it feels alien, e.g. feeling a lack of connection and fulfilment in work
Alternative ideology	An **ideology** different from that of the **ruling class** but not in opposition to it
Apostasy	Abandoning your religious beliefs
Artefacts	In science, phenomena that are produced as a result of the process of studying something and which did not occur naturally
Ascetic lifestyle	Involves forgoing life's pleasures such as drinking, dancing, sex outside marriage and consuming luxury goods
Audience cults	Groups which believe in supernatural phenomena, but have minimal contact with their followers, require little commitment and often act as little more than a form of entertainment. Examples include astrology
Black feminist	A feminist who believes that inequalities based upon **ethnicity** and gender work together to create particular disadvantages for black women
Bourgeoisie	The **ruling class** in **capitalism** who own property such as capital, businesses and shares
Breadwinner	The person in a household who does the most paid work
Bureaucracy	An organisation in which people follow rules and which is run through a **hierarchy** of paid workers
Capital	Assets that can be used to produce more resources
Capitalist society/ capitalism	A society in which people are employed for wages and businesses are set up with the aim of making a profit
Causal relationship	When one factor is at least the partial result of another
Census	A social survey carried out by the government every ten years in the UK that collects standardised data about the whole of the population
Charismatic leader	Someone who commands support by virtue of their personality alone
Church	A large religious organisation, which traditionally claims a monopoly of the religious truth and is tied to the **state** in a particular society. It tries to be universal, i.e. to include all members of society
Civilisation	In Huntington's theory, there are six civilisations in the world partly defined by their religious beliefs (Western, Confucian, Japanese, Islamic, Hindu, Slavic-Orthodox, Latin American and African), which have quite different lifestyles and tend to clash when they come into contact
Civil religion	Durkheim saw nationalism as a civil religion because it served the same **functions** as traditional religions, i.e. it integrated groups of people with a shared set of beliefs
Class/social class	Groups within society distinguished by their economic position and who are therefore unequal, e.g. the middle class in better paid non-manual jobs and the working class in less well-paid physical jobs
Class consciousness	When a **social class** becomes aware of its own true interests and begins to act to further those interests

Class subculture	The distinctive lifestyle associated with a particular **class**
Client cults	Spiritual/religious groups that offer services to followers without requiring them to follow a set of beliefs in the same way as a conventional religion. They offer followers a way of enhancing their existing lives rather than an alternative lifestyle. Followers are often seen as customers. Examples are Scientology and Transcendental Meditation (TM)
Cohort	A group of people born in the same time period or joining an organisation at the same time
Collective conscience	To Durkheim, the shared morality of a society
Collectivist	Putting the interests of the social group before the interests of the individual
Commune	A place where a number of individuals, most of whom are likely to be unrelated by blood or marriage, live together
Communism	A political philosophy supported by Karl Marx and others, which advocates the creation of classless, egalitarian societies based upon the abolition of private ownership of the **means of production**
Competition	When individuals or businesses try to do better than one another, e.g. by selling more goods than another company
Conflict	Any clashes between individuals or groups who have different aims or interests, ranging from arguments to wars
Conflict theory	Theory of society, which sees one or more groups in competition for scarce or valued goods; examples include Marxism and feminism
Congregational domain	The environment in which traditional **churches** and **denominations** exist, i.e. formal organisations with periodic, usually weekly, attendance at services for the purposes of prayer
Consensus theory	Theory of society, which assumes that the same interests are shared across society meaning that there is little conflict
Conservative force	Something that prevents change and/or supports traditional beliefs and **values**
Consumer culture	**Culture** based around the purchase and use of consumer goods
Consumption	Buying and using consumer goods
Correlation	A statistical tendency for two things to be found together
Counterculture	The beliefs and lifestyle of a group who are opposed to a dominant culture
Counter-school culture	The beliefs of the group who are opposed to the **values** of those in authority at a school
Cult movements	Groups which dominate the lives of their followers but do not have the conventional belief system of a religion (such as a belief in God). They may have supernatural or spiritual beliefs. An example is the Heaven's Gate cult
Cults	Small religious or spiritual organisations which may not have a belief in a traditional God and tend to exist in less tension with the wider society than **sects**
Cultural defence	Using religion as a way of protecting identity in an essentially hostile environment
Cultural transition	Where religion is used to cope with the upheaval of migration
Culture	The **norms**, **values**, attitudes and lifestyle of a social group

Dedifferentiation	A reduction in the significance of differences between categories of things or the blurring of the boundaries between those categories
Deduction/deductive approach	Making predictions based upon a theory
Denomination	A medium-sized religious organisation that has broken away from a larger **church**; it is respectable but has no connection with the **state**
Denotative language-games	Conversation or discussion based on the premise that an attempt is being made to find the truth
Deterministic	A theory, which sees behaviour as entirely determined by external circumstances, leaving the individual with little or no choice about how they behave
Deviant	Contradicting the norms of society
Differential socialisation	The way that different groups are brought up, e.g. different genders
Discourse analysis	Analysis of the meaning of texts to reveal the message behind them, based on the view that **power** can result from having a particular way of talking about a subject to be accepted in society
Disenchantment	According to Weber, the process by which the modern world loses religious faith and belief in the supernatural and magic
Disengagement	The withdrawal of the **church** from the wider society
Division of labour	The way in which jobs are divided up between two or more people, e.g. who does particular tasks in a society
Dual consciousness	In **neo-Marxist** theory, a set of beliefs that are partly shaped by **ruling class ideology** but also partly see through it because of the experience of **exploitation**
Economic base	In Marxist theory, the foundation of society consisting of the economic system
Economic capital	Material assets such as housing and income, which can be helpful in achieving success in life
Efficiency	Achieving the best possible outcomes using the least possible resources
Elect (the)	In Calvinism, those people who were predestined to go to heaven
Emergent ideology	The **ideology** of a **class** that is developing and growing in importance
Ethnic group/ ethnicity	A group within a population regarded by themselves or by others as culturally distinctive; they usually see themselves as having a common origin
Evolution	The process whereby organisms change very gradually over time as they adapt to their environments
Exploitation	One group treating another group unfairly in order to benefit themselves
External stimuli	Factors outside of the individual mind, which humans become aware of through their senses and which might affect their behaviour
False class consciousness	The mistaken beliefs held by a **subject class** that society is fair and just and a failure to realise that they are being **exploited**
Falsifying	Proving something wrong
Fascism	A political **ideology** based on a form of authoritarian, dictatorial nationalism

Feudalism	An economic system in **pre-industrial societies**, particularly in Europe, in which land was owned by feudal lords, and serfs had to work the land for them and hand over a proportion of their produce
Fragmented	Divided into small pieces so that no coherent whole exists
Free market	A system in which businesses can compete with one another without state interference
Function	A useful job performed by an institution for society
Functional definitions	Definitions of religion based on the social role it performs, e.g. integrating society
Functionalism	A sociological perspective, which believes that social institutions serve some positive purpose
Fundamentalism	A set of religious beliefs, which claims to go back to the fundamentals of a religion and which often claims that other versions of that religion have become distorted and watered-down or diluted
Gender roles	The socially expected behaviour of men and women in a particular society
Gender socialisation	The way in which males and females are taught to behave differently in a particular society
Generalisability	How reasonable it is to make statements about a wider **population** on the basis of a particular **sample**
Generalised	To Parsons, the process whereby beliefs specific to one area of social life (particularly religion) seep into all areas of social life, e.g. the way Christian values have become part of general values in American society
Globalisation	The process by which the significance of distance or space between places and the importance of national boundaries both become less significant, so that the world becomes essentially one single, large place
Hegemony/ hegemonic	Political or cultural dominance
Hierarchy	Where individuals are ranked above and below one another and orders and instructions flow from the top of the hierarchy down to the bottom
Holistic milieu	Environment in which **New Age** beliefs flourish, including encounter groups, private consultations with therapists, shops, festivals and gatherings. Holistic refers to the emphasis on the whole person present in the spirituality of the New Age
Human potential movement	Movement closely associated with the **New Age** concerned with allowing people to develop to their maximum potential, particularly in terms of their spirituality but also in other aspects of their lives such as the ability to be effective workers
Idealism	A belief that developments in society can be shaped by people's ideas rather than just by material forces (see **materialism**)
Identity	The way you see yourself and/or are seen by others
Ideology	A distorted set of beliefs that favours the interests of a particular social group
Inclusive	A definition of religion, which includes a broad range of belief systems, rather than more restricted definitions, which only include belief systems that involve a belief in the supernatural, e.g. beliefs could include nationalism or even support of a football team

Individualism/ individualist	An emphasis on the desires or interests of individual people rather than those of wider social groups
Induction	Producing a theory through an examination of empirical evidence
Industrialisation	The process whereby manufacturing takes over from agriculture as the most important component in a society's economy
Industrial society	A society that has undergone the process of industrialisation
Infrastructure	In Marxist theory, the foundation of society consisting of the economic system (same as the **economic base)**
Internal stimuli	Factors within the human mind such as beliefs, emotions, **meanings** and **motives**, which might affect a person's behaviour
Interview	A research method in which one or more people ask an individual or group a series of questions
Islamophobia	Stereotypical and distorted fear and prejudice directed towards Muslims
Laissez-faire capitalism	A **capitalist** system with a strong emphasis on the **free market** and lack of government interference in the economy
Laws	Statements about universal relationships of cause and effect
Legitimate	(verb) To make something seem fair and reasonable (noun) Something that is accepted as fair and reasonable
Liberal feminism	A version of feminism, which is relatively moderate and believes that the position of women in society can be improved through reform rather than radical or revolutionary change
Liberation theology	A version of the Roman Catholic religion in Latin America, in which the church sides with the poor and seeks to overcome their poverty, e.g. through the redistribution of land from the rich to the poor
Life crisis	A period in which a person's life is in turmoil due to dramatic changes taking place such as the death of a relative or the transition to adulthood
Logic in use	The actual procedures that are used by scientists rather than the procedures that they claim to use (**reconstructed logics**)
Manual labour/ manual jobs	Work that primarily involves physical effort rather than thought
Marginal	On the fringes of society with little stake or **power** within it
Marxist	A person who follows the theories of Karl Marx, which argue that society is dominated by a **ruling class** that owns the **means of production**
Masculinity	The behaviour and social roles expected of men in a particular culture
Materialism	A belief that the development of societies is driven by material forces such as developments in production, technology and the economy
Meanings	The interpretations made by people of acts, words or other symbols
Means of production	Those things required to produce goods such as land machinery, capital, technical knowledge and workers
Mechanical solidarity	According to Durkheim, the type of **social solidarity** based upon similarity between people and typical of **pre-industrial societies**

Metanarrative	In **postmodern** theory, a big story that tells people how the world works, how they should behave and what should be done to improve society. Examples include religions, political **ideologies** and **scientific rationalism**
Metaphysical stage	According to Comte, a stage in human history in which philosophical beliefs were dominant
Middle class	People who have white-collar jobs that require some qualifications and are generally better paid than the **working class**
Middle-ground new religious movements	Religious/spiritual organisations, which fall somewhere in between those that are **world-rejecting**, **world-accommodating** and **world-affirming**
Mode of production	A system of producing things, which dominates society, e.g. **capitalism**
Modernisation	The process of becoming more modern or moving towards **modernity**
Modernity	An era in the development of society characterised by a belief in **scientific rationalism**, the decline of **religion** and a belief in progress
Monotheistic	Believing in a single God
Motives	The subjective reasons for behaving in particular ways
Natural selection	The process in **evolution** whereby those that are not naturally well adapted to their environment die out, and those that are well adapted survive and have offspring
Neo-liberalism	A belief in the superiority of the free market as a way of organising society over other principles of organisation
Neo-Marxism	New versions of **Marxism** that are strongly influenced by the works of Karl Marx but disagree with some aspects of them and have been updated to fit contemporary society
New Age movement	Belief systems with a spiritual element that are not organised in traditional ways and allow individuals considerable freedom of choice about what combination of beliefs they might have. It can involve alternative therapies, belief in the supernatural or the practising of techniques to achieve spiritual fulfilment
New religious movement (NRM)	A religious or spiritual organisation emerging during the 1960s and 1970s
Non-manual labour	Work that does not primarily require physical effort, e.g. office work
Non-representative sampling	A sampling technique in which people who are not typical of a wider **population** are chosen
Nontrinitarian	Christian religious organisations that are not based on a belief in the Holy Trinity
Norms	Specific, informal rules of behaviour in a particular society
Objectivity	Making truthful statements about the world, which are not influenced by personal opinion or preferences
Official statistics	Numerical data produced by government agencies
Oppositional ideology	An **ideology** directly opposed to that of the **ruling class**
Organic solidarity	To Durkheim, the type of **social solidarity** found in **modern** industrial societies based upon interdependence between those with specialist but different **roles** where there is a **division of labour**

Orientalism	According to Said, a discourse, common in Western societies, which betrays those from Eastern societies (or the Orient) as exotic, strange and often rather untrustworthy
Other	A person or group who is different from the group with which someone identifies; they are seen as abnormal because they deviate from an assumed norm and this difference may be seen as threatening
Paradigm	A whole theory or way of looking at something, particularly within science, that governs the way that data is collected and interpreted
Patriarchy	Literally 'rule by the father', usually used by feminists to refer to a system in which men have more **power** than women and shape how societies are run
Peer group	A group of people with a similar **status** and often age to whom you compare yourself and who may exercise influence on your behaviour
Period effect	When people born in a particular time period are significantly different from those born in other time periods due to the particular experiences that they share, e.g. living through a major war or other significant events or social changes
Pluralistically legitimate	Only one of several sets of beliefs accepted as reasonable within the society
Political ideology	A set of political beliefs that can be seen as supporting the interests of one group in society
Polytheistic	Believing in several gods
Population	The total group the sociologist is interested in when conducting research
Positivism	A philosophy of social research based upon scientific ideas of **objectivity**
Positivist stage	According to Comte, a stage in human history in which scientific beliefs have become dominant
Postmodern	Belonging to or typical of **postmodernity**
Postmodernism	The theory that society is moving or has moved to a new stage in which **scientific rationality** has lost its central importance, people no longer believe in **metanarratives** and their **identities** become more fluid
Postmodernist	A follower of the theory of **postmodernism**
Postmodernity	The period following **modernity** that **postmodernists** believe we have entered or are entering
Power	The ability of a person to get their own way or to determine outcomes regardless of the wishes of others
Prediction	Making statements about what you believe will happen in the future
Pre-industrial society	Societies that existed before industrialisation, in which most production was based on agriculture
Primary socialisation	The first stage of the process through which children learn the culture of their society; it takes place in the family
Private sphere	Areas of social life involved with personal and family life that are not usually open to public view
Privatised	In secularisation theory, moving from the **public sphere** to the **private sphere**

Profane	Things that have no special sacred significance, the ordinary and everyday
Protestant ethic	In Weber's work, the attitude of some Protestant groups who believed that in working hard they were doing God's will and fulfilling their calling
Public sphere	Areas of social life that are open to participation or scrutiny by people in the population in general, as opposed to the **private sphere**
Questionnaire	A written list of questions
Racism	Discriminatory beliefs or actions based upon a person's supposed 'race' or ethnic group
Radical feminist	A feminist who believes that the primary division in society is between men and women and that the **exploitation** of women by men is the central feature of society. They seek major changes in society to correct the situation
Radical force	Something that encourages change, particularly rapid or major change
Rational/rationality/ rational action	Acting in ways that are calculated as the best means to achieve particular ends and avoid emotion
Rationalisation	The process of becoming more rational
Reconstructed logics	Procedures that scientists say they use, which may be very different from actual **logics in use**
Relative autonomy	In Marxist theory, a degree of independence, particularly when parts of the **superstructure** have some independence from the **economic base** and the **ruling class**
Relative deprivation	A sense of feeling deprived compared to others with whom one compares oneself
Reliability	Data is reliable if another researcher using identical methods would produce the same results
Religion	Usually seen as a belief system involving a belief in a supernatural being or forces beyond the level of ordinary experience. May or may not claim the existence of a supreme God or several gods. Definitions of religion may be **inclusive** or **exclusive**, **functional** or **substantive**
Religious pluralism	The existence of many different religions within a single society
Renewed vigour	To Chryssides, the reassertion of religious belief and the strengthening of it in response to migration or hostility towards the beliefs of a minority **ethnic group**
Representativeness	How typical data is of a wider **population**
Resacrilisation	A renewed emphasis upon the importance of the **sacred**
Residual ideology	The **ideology** of a declining **class**
Respectable	Accepted within the society as conforming to its **norms** and **values**
Risk	The possibility that significantly detrimental events may take place, though risk often implies some gain if the possibility of harm is faced and avoided
Roles	Positions in society that are associated with accepted patterns of behaviour
Ruling class	In Marxist theory, the group who are dominant in society by virtue of their wealth and power

Ruling class ideology	The belief system in a society which reflects the interests of the **ruling class** by **legitimating** their dominance in society
Sacred	Things that are given a special meaning and significance and treated with awe, veneration and respect, e.g. religious beliefs and symbols
Sample	A group selected from within a wider **population** with whom research is carried out
Science	The systematic and (supposedly) objective study of the natural world
Scientific rationalism	A belief system based upon the principle that it is possible to understand the natural world **objectively** and on this basis plan in order to achieve goals in the most efficient way possible. Scientific rationalism supports the belief that humans can ensure progress through their planning and calculation
Sects	Small religious organisations with values that are at odds with or hostile to the wider society; sometimes seen as groups breaking away from existing religions
Secularisation	In general terms, the process through which religion declines over time. Some definitions stress the role of religion in society, and others the strength of personal belief and participation
Sex stereotyping	Treating males and females according to widely held stereotypes of their typical behaviour.
Social control	The mechanisms through which society prevents people from breaking the **norms** and laws of society through both formal mechanisms, such as the legal system, and informal mechanisms, such as disapproval and gossip
Social differentiation	The development of different spheres of social life
Social facts	True statements about social phenomena
Socialisation	The process through which people learn the culture of their society
Socialist feminist	A feminist who believes that **class** inequality and **patriarchy** work together to shape the structure of society
Social solidarity	A sense of belonging, commitment and loyalty to a social group
Social structure	The overall way that society is organised, involving relationships between the major institutions
Spirit of capitalism	In Weber's work, the desire to reinvest profits to create more and more profit in the future rather than spend money on personal consumption
Spiritual revolution	According to Heelas and Woodhead, a process whereby traditional religious beliefs existing in the **congregational domain** are gradually replaced in importance by the growth of beliefs in the **holistic milieu**
Spiritual shoppers	People who look around for new spiritual ideas, often frequently changing them and sometimes mixing different ideas together, thought to be typical of the **New Age**
State	The practices and institutions directly or indirectly controlled by the government and its bureaucracy in a country
Status	The amount of esteem in which people are held by others in society
Strong religion	Religion which exercises a powerful influence over the lives of its followers

Structural differentiation	The development of a more complex social structure with a greater range of institutions carrying out specialist tasks, e.g. the development of a welfare state in which institutions such as health and social services replace jobs previously carried out by the family or by religion.
Structural location	The way your position in the structure of society affects your behaviour
Subculture	A group within a wider culture, which has significantly different **norms**, attitudes, **values** and lifestyle to other groups in society while sharing some aspects of the wider culture
Subject class	In Marxist theory, the group in society who are exploited by the **ruling class** whom they have to work for because they lack the **capital** to produce goods for themselves
Subjective	Based upon personal opinion rather than **objective** evidence
Subjectivisation	A movement in society towards an increasing emphasis upon subjective feeling and opinion and away from faith in **objectivity,** e.g. faith in **science**
Substantive definition	Definitions of religion based on the contents of the religious beliefs, e.g. belief in a god or gods, or belief in the supernatural
Superstructure	In Marxist theory, the non-economic parts of society such as the family, which are shaped by the economy and controlled by the **ruling class**
Survey	Research collecting standardised information about a large group of people
Survival of the fittest	The process whereby only those organisms that are well adapted to their environment survive and those which are weak, or poorly adapted, die
Technical language games	Conversation or discussion based upon the premise that knowledge sought should be useful rather than necessarily truthful
Theodicy of disprivilege	A set of religious beliefs that help the poor and oppressed to cope with their situation
Theological stage	According to Comte, a stage in human history in which religious beliefs were dominant
Total institution	An organisation, which completely dominates the lives of those who are part of it, e.g. some **sects**, prisons, military ships, concentration camps and boarding schools
Typology	A classification of different types of a phenomenon
Uniquely legitimate	Seen as the only true set of beliefs
Universal	Found in all societies
Upper class	The highest **social class** in society, consisting of those who own wealth or property
Validity	How true data is, i.e. how close the fit is between the data and reality
Value consensus	According to Parsons, the general agreement found in society about what is right and wrong
Value-laden	Beliefs influenced by personal opinions about right and wrong
Values	General beliefs about what is right or wrong in a particular society
Weak religion	Religion, which does not exercise a strong influence over the lives of its followers
Wealth	Money or saleable possessions owned by an individual social group

Working class	People who do manual jobs that require relatively few qualifications and are usually less well-paid than **middle-class** jobs
World-accommodating new religious movements	Religious groups emerging since the 1960s in which people take their religious beliefs very seriously but carry on with normal lives within society when they are not practising their religion
World-affirming new religious movements	Religious/spiritual groups emerging since the 1960s in which members use what they learn from the group to enhance their lives within mainstream society
World-rejecting new religious movements	Religious groups emerging since the 1960s in which members turn away from life within mainstream society and adopt **behaviour** and **values** at odds with those of the **norm**

Index